LANGUAGE AND MYTH

Originally published in German as Number VI of the
"Studien der Bibliothek Warburg," under the
editorship of Fritz Saxl.

LANGUAGE and MYTH

By ERNST CASSIRER

LATE VISITING PROFESSOR OF PHILOSOPHY
COLUMBIA UNIVERSITY

TRANSLATED BY
SUSANNE K. LANGER
AUTHOR OF
Philosophy in a New Key

DOVER PUBLICATIONS INC.

Dedicated to my Father-in-Law,

OTTO BONDY,

upon the occasion of his

eightieth birthday.

E. C.

TRANSLATOR'S PREFACE

TWENTY-TWO years ago, Ernst Cassirer published the first volume of a work which struck a new note in so-called "theory of knowledge." It was called *Die Philosophie der Symbolischen Formen* (*The Philosophy of Symbolic Forms*). In this work, the "theory of knowledge" became a theory of *mental activity*, which gave as minute and scholarly attention to the forms of feeling and imagination as to the categories of sense perception and logic.

The book has not yet been translated into English; the only access we have to his ideas, therefore, is his recent small volume, *An Essay on Man*, which presents his main conclusions in brief résumé. But to be presented with a thinker's conclusions, not really seeing the path whereby he reached them, or knowing the first suggestion—the insight or naïve perception—which opened that path, is unsatisfactory to anyone whose philosophical interest is more than skin deep.

Now fortunately, at the time when Professor Cassirer was engrossed in the first half of his great work—tracing the story of human mentality *before* the birth of that rather abstract form of conception which we call "logic" —he wrote a short but faithful account of his growing idea, his theory of myth and language. This little study, entitled *Sprache und Mythos*, reveals the genesis of some of those great conclusions for which he is known to the world; it gives one a look into the mental laboratory where new ideas are generated and developed.

Americans like to look into laboratories, especially when they know that something big is in the making there. So this philosophical fragment which prepares a whole world view is here presented to the English-speaking public, for the same reason that the Bibliothek Warburg (one of the world's great ventures in popular education) saw fit to publish it originally.

But an expert in his sanctum sometimes appears to make strange moves, unless we know what he is trying to do. A layman seriously watching him may well appreciate a tip to that effect from some fellow worker in the place. Therefore I may be permitted to point out in advance what Professor Cassirer was undertaking, and how he proposed to do it.

He was originally struck with the fact that the "theory of knowledge," as philosophers had developed it since the Middle Ages, concerned itself solely with the appreciation of "facts" and the development of orderly thought about facts. The inveterate belief of all mankind in myth, sometimes crystallized into dogmas, sometimes degraded into vulgar superstition, was always excluded from the field of philosophical interest, either as divine revelation, which philosophy could not touch, or (especially in modern times) as a miscarriage of logical explanation, a product of ignorance. But the whole realm of mythical concepts is too great a phenomenon to be accounted for as a "mistake" due to the absence of logically recorded facts. Mere ignorance should be agnostic—empty and negative—not exciting and irrepressible. And it dawned on the philosopher that *theory of mind* might well begin not with the analysis of knowledge, but with a search for the reason and spiritual function of this peculiar sort of "ignorance."

Here he was helped by a stroke of insight: the realization that *language*, man's prime instrument of reason, reflects his mythmaking tendency more than his rationalizing tendency. Language, the symbolization of thought, exhibits two entirely different modes of thought. Yet in both modes the mind is powerful and creative. It expresses itself in different forms, one of which is discursive logic, the other creative imagination.

Human intelligence begins with *conception*, the prime mental activity; the process of conception always culminates in *symbolic expression*. A conception is fixed and held only when it has been embodied in a symbol. So the study of symbolic forms offers a key to the forms of human conception. The genesis of symbolic forms—verbal, religious, artistic, mathematical, or whatever modes of expression there be—is the odyssey of the mind.

The two oldest of these modes seem to be language and myth. Since both are of prehistoric birth, we cannot fix the age of either; but there are many reasons for regarding them as twin creatures. The intuitions about nature and man reflected in the oldest verbal roots, and the processes by which language probably grew up are the same elementary intuitions and the same processes which are expressed in the development of myths. They are not the categories and canons of so-called "discursive logic," the forms of reason, which underlie both common sense and science. Reason is not man's primitive endowment, but his *achievement*. The seeds of it—fertile, yet long dormant—lie in language; logic springs from language when that greatest of symbolic modes is mature (as it is by the time we meet it in history or ethnology).

Myth never breaks out of the magic circle of its figurative ideas. It reaches religious and poetic heights; but the gulf between its conceptions and those of science never narrows the least bit. But language, born in that same magic circle, has the power to break its bounds; language takes us from the mythmaking phase of human mentality to the phase of logical thought and the conception of facts.

Theory of knowledge has always treated this final achievement as man's natural and primitive way of thinking, and taken "facts" as his earliest stock in trade. Consequently, it could find no connection at all between myth and truth, poetry and common sense, religion and science; most of man's actual ideas, most of his cultural and spiritual background, had to be discounted as error, caprice, or emotional indulgence. Professor Cassirer's great thesis, based on the evidence of language and verified by his sources with quite thrilling success, is that *philosophy of mind involves much more than a theory of knowledge; it involves a theory of prelogical conception and expression, and their final culmination in reason and factual knowledge.*

Such a view changes our whole picture of human mentality. The following pages give the reader the high lights of significant fact which suggested, supported, and finally clinched the theory. I offer the translation of this little study (with some slight modifications and abridgments made by the author shortly before his death) both as a statement of a new philosophical insight and as a revelation of the philosopher's work: his material, his technique, and the solution of the problem by a final flash of interpretive genius.

S. K. L.

New York City
November 1, 1945

CONTENTS

LANGUAGE AND MYTH

The Place of Language
and Myth in the Pattern of
Human Culture

THE opening passage of the Platonic dialogue *Phaedrus* describes how Socrates lets Phaedrus, whom he encounters, lure him beyond the gates of the city to the banks of Ilissus. Plato has pictured the setting of this scene in nicest detail, and there lies over it a glamour and fragrance well-nigh unequaled in classical descriptions of nature. In the shade of a tall plane tree, at the brink of a cool spring, Socrates and Phaedrus lie down; the summer breeze is mild and sweet and full of the cicada's song. In the midst of this landscape Phaedrus raises the question whether this be not the place where, according to a myth, Boreas carried off the fair Orithyia; for the water is clear and translucent here, fitting for maidens to sport in and bathe. Socrates, when pressed with questions as to whether he believes this tale, this "mythologemen," replies that, although he cannot be said to believe it, yet he is not at a loss as to its significance. "For," he says, "then I could proceed as do the learned, and say by way of clever interpretation, that Orithyia, while playing with her companion Pharmacia, had been borne over yonder cliffs by Boreas the Northwind, and because of this manner of her death she was said to have been carried off by the god Boreas. . . . But I," he adds, "for my part, Phaedrus, I find that sort of thing pretty enough, yet consider such interpretations rather an artificial and tedious business, and do not envy him who indulges in it. For he will necessarily have to account for centaurs and the chimaera, too, and will find himself overwhelmed by a very multitude of such creatures, gorgons and pegasuses and countless other strange monsters. And whoever discredits all these wonderful beings and tackles them with the intention of reducing them each to some probability, will have to devote a great deal of time to this bootless sort of wisdom. But I have no leisure at all for such pastimes, and the reason, my dear friend, is that as yet I cannot, as the Delphic precept has it, know myself. So it seems absurd to me that, as long as I am in ignorance of myself, I should concern myself about extraneous matters. Therefore I let all such things be as they may, and think not of them, but of myself—whether I be, indeed, a creature more complex and monstrous than Typhon, or whether perchance I be a gentler and simpler animal, whose nature contains a divine and noble essence." (*Phaedrus*, 229D ff.)

This sort of myth interpretation, which the Sophists and Rhetoricians of the time held in high repute as the flower of polite learning and the height of the urbane spirit, seemed to Plato the very opposite of this spirit; but although he denounced it as such, calling it a rustic science (ἄγροικος σοφία), his judgment did not prevent the learned from indulging in this sort of wisdom for centuries to come. As the Sophists and Rhetoricians vied with each other at this intellectual sport in Plato's day, so the Stoics and Neoplatonists did in the Hellenistic period. And it was ever and always the science of language, of etymology, that served as a vehicle for such research. Here in the realm of spooks and daemons, as well as in the higher reaches of mythology, the Faustian word seemed ever to hold good: here it was always assumed that the essence of each mythical figure could be directly learned from its name. The notion that name and essence bear a necessary and internal relation to each other, that the name does not merely denote but actually is the essence of its object, that the potency of the real thing is contained in the name—that is one of the fundamental assumptions of the mythmaking consciousness itself. Philosophical and scientific *mythology*, too, seemed to accept this assumption. What in the spirit of myth itself functions as a living and immediate conviction becomes a postulate of reflective procedure for the science of mythology; the doctrine of the intimate relation between names and essences, and of their latent identity, is here set up as a methodological principle.

Among the philosophers it was especially Herbert Spencer who tried to prove the thesis that the mythico-religious veneration of natural phenomena, as, for instance, the sun and the moon, has its ultimate origin in nothing more than a misinterpretation of the *names* which men have applied to these objects. Among the philologists, Max Müller has taken the method of philological analysis not only as a means to reveal the nature of certain mythical beings, especially in the context of Vedic religion, but also as a point of departure for his general theory of the connection between language and myth. For him, myth is neither a transformation of history into fabulous legend nor is it fable accepted as history; and just as certainly it does not spring directly from the contemplation of the great forms and powers of nature. What we call myth is, for him, something conditioned and negotiated by the agency of language; it is, in fact, the product of a basic shortcoming, an inherent weakness of language. All linguistic denotation is essentially ambiguous—and in this ambiguity, this "paronymia" of words lies the source of all myths. The examples by which Max Müller supports this theory are characteristic of his approach. He cites, as one instance, the legend of Deucalion and Pyrrha, who, after Zeus had rescued them from the great flood which destroyed mankind, became the ancestors of a new race by taking up *stones* and casting them over their shoulders, whereupon the stones became men. This origin of human beings from stones is simply absurd and seems to defy all interpretation—but is it not immediately clarified as we recall the fact that in Greek men and stones are denoted by identical or at least similar sounding *names*, that the words λαοί and λᾶας are assonant? Or take the myth of Daphne, who is saved from Apollo's embraces by the fact that her mother, the Earth, transforms her into a laurel tree. Again it is only the history of language that can make this myth "comprehensible," and give it any sort of sense. Who was Daphne? In order to answer this question we must resort to etymology, that is to say, we must investigate the history of the word. "Daphne" can be traced back to the Sanskrit *Ahanâ*, and *Ahanâ* means in Sanskrit the redness of dawn. As soon as we know this, the whole matter becomes clear. The story of Phoebus and Daphne is nothing but a description of what one may observe every day: first, the appearance of the dawnlight in the eastern sky, then the rising of the sun-god who hastens after his bride, then the gradual fading of the red dawn at the touch of the fiery rays, and finally its death or disappearance in the bosom of Mother Earth. So the decisive condition for the development of the myth was not the natural phenomenon itself, but rather the circumstance that the Greek word for the laurel (δάφνη) and the Sanskrit word for the dawn are related; this entails with a sort of logical necessity the identification of the beings they denote. This, therefore, is his conclusion:

"Mythology is inevitable, it is natural, it is an inherent necessity of language, if we recognize in language the outward form and manifestation of thought; it is in fact the dark shadow which language throws upon thought, and which can never disappear till language becomes entirely commensurate with thought, which it never will. Mythology, no doubt, breaks out more fiercely during the early periods of the history of human thought, but it never disappears altogether. Depend upon it, there is mythology now as there was in the time of Homer, only we do not perceive it, because we ourselves live in the very shadow of it, and because we all shrink from the full meridian light of truth. . . . Mythology, in the highest sense, is the power exercised by language on thought in every possible sphere of mental activity."[1]

It might seem an idle pursuit to hark back to such points of view, which have long been abandoned by the etymology and comparative mythological research of to-day, were it not for the fact that this standpoint represents a typical attitude which is ever recurrent in all related fields, in mythology as in linguistic studies, in theory of art as well as in theory of knowledge. For Max Müller the mythical world is essentially a world of illusion—but an illusion that finds its explanation whenever the original, necessary self-deception of the mind, from which the error arises, is discovered. This self-

---

[1] Max Müller, "The Philosophy of Mythology," appended to *Introduction to the Science of Religion* (London, 1873), pp. 353-355.

deception is rooted in language, which is forever making
game of the human mind, ever ensnaring it in that
iridescent play of meanings that is its own heritage. And
this notion that myth does not rest upon a positive
power of formulation and creation, but rather upon a
mental *defect*—that we find in it a "pathological" influence of speech—this notion has its proponents even in
modern ethnological literature.[2]

But when we reduce it to its philosophical lowest
terms, this attitude turns out to be simply the logical result of that naïve realism which regards the reality of objects as something directly and unequivocally given,
literally something tangible—ἀπρίξ ταῖν χεροῖν, as Plato
says. If reality is conceived in this manner, then of course
everything which has not this solid sort of reality dis-
solves into mere fraud and illusion. This illusion may be
ever so finely wrought, and flit about us in the gayest and
loveliest colors; the fact remains that this image has no
independent content, no intrinsic meaning. It does indeed reflect a reality—but a reality to which it can never
measure up, and which it can never adequately portray.
From this point of view all artistic creation becomes a
mere imitation, which must always fall short of the
original. Not only simple imitation of a sensibly presented model, but also what is known as idealization,
manner, or style, must finally succumb to this verdict;
for measured by the naked "truth" of the object to be
depicted, idealization itself is nothing but subjective
misconception and falsification. And it seems that all
other processes of mental gestation involve the same sort
of outrageous distortion, the same departure from objective reality and the immediate data of experience.

[2] E.g., B. Brinton, *Religions of Primitive Peoples* (New York and
London, 1907), pp. 115 ff.

For all mental processes fail to grasp reality itself, and in order to represent it, to hold it at all, they are driven to the use of symbols. But all symbolism harbors the curse of mediacy; it is bound to obscure what it seeks to reveal. Thus the sound of *speech* strives to "express" subjective and objective happening, the "inner" and the "outer" world; but what of this it can retain is not the life and individual fullness of existence, but only a dead abbreviation of it. All that "denotation" to which the spoken word lays claim is really nothing more than mere suggestion; a "suggestion" which, in face of the concrete variegation and totality of actual experience, must always appear a poor and empty shell. That is true of the external as well as the inner world: "When *speaks* the soul, alas, the *soul* no longer speaks!"

From this point it is but a single step to the conclusion which the modern skeptical critics of language have drawn: the complete dissolution of any alleged truth content of language, and the realization that this content is nothing but a sort of phantasmagoria of the spirit. Moreover, from this standpoint, not only myth, art, and language, but even theoretical knowledge itself becomes a phantasmagoria; for even knowledge can never reproduce the true nature of things as they are, but must frame their essence in "concepts." But what are concepts save formulations and creations of thought, which, instead of giving us the true forms of objects, show us rather the forms of thought itself? Consequently all schemata which science evolves in order to classify, organize, and summarize the phenomena of the real world turn out to be nothing but arbitrary schemes— airy fabrics of the mind, which express not the nature of things, but the nature of mind. So knowledge, as well as myth, language, and art, has been reduced to a kind of fiction—to a fiction that recommends itself by its use-fulness, but must not be measured by any strict standard of truth, if it is not to melt away into nothingness.

Against this self-dissolution of the spirit there is only one remedy: to accept in all seriousness what Kant calls his "Copernican revolution." Instead of measuring the content, meaning, and truth of intellectual forms by something extraneous which is supposed to be repro-duced in them, we must find in these forms themselves the measure and criterion for their truth and intrinsic meaning. Instead of taking them as mere copies of some-thing else, we must see in each of these spiritual forms a spontaneous law of generation; an original way and tendency of expression which is more than a mere record of something initially given in fixed categories of real existence. From this point of view, myth, art, language and science appear as symbols; not in the sense of mere figures which refer to some given reality by means of suggestion and allegorical renderings, but in the sense of forces each of which produces and posits a world of its own. In these realms the spirit exhibits itself in that inwardly determined dialectic by virtue of which alone there is any reality, any organized and definite Being at all. Thus the special symbolic forms are not imitations, but *organs* of reality, since it is solely by their agency that anything real becomes an object for intellectual apprehension, and as such is made visible to us. The question as to what reality is apart from these forms, and what are its independent attributes, becomes irrelevant here. For the mind, only that can be visible which has some definite form; but every form of existence has its source in some peculiar way of seeing, some intellectual formulation and intuition of meaning. Once language, myth, art and science are recognized as such ideational forms, the basic philosophical question is no longer that of their relation to an absolute reality which forms, so to speak, their solid and substantial substratum; the central problem now is that of their mutual limitation and supplementation. Though they all function organically together in the construction of spiritual reality, yet each of these organs has its individual assignment.

From this angle, the relation between language and myth also appears in a new light. It is no longer a matter of simply deriving one of these phenomena from the other, of "explaining" it in terms of the other—for that would be to level them both, to rob them of their characteristic features. If myth be really, as Max Müller's theory has it, nothing but the darkening shadow which language throws upon thought, it is mystifying indeed that this shadow should appear ever as in an aura of its own light, should evolve a positive vitality and activity of its own, which tends to eclipse what we commonly call the immediate reality of *things*, so that even the wealth of empirical, sensuous experience pales before it. As Wilhelm von Humboldt has said in connection with the language problem: "Man lives with his objects chiefly—in fact, since his feeling and acting depends on his perceptions, one may say exclusively—as language presents them to him. By the same process whereby he spins language out of his own being, he ensnares himself in it; and each language draws a magic circle round the people to which it belongs, a circle from which there is no escape save by stepping out of it into another."[3]

This holds, perhaps, even more for the basic mythical conceptions of mankind than for language. Such conceptions are not culled from a ready-made world of

[3] W. von Humboldt, *Einleitung zum Kawi-Werk*, S.W. (Coll. ed.), VII, 60.

Being, they are not mere products of fantasy which vapor off from fixed, empirical, realistic existence, to float above the actual world like a bright mist; to primitive consciousness they present the *totality* of Being. The mythical form of conception is not something superadded to certain definite *elements* of empirical existence; instead, the primary "experience" itself is steeped in the imagery of myth and saturated with its atmosphere. Man lives with *objects* only in so far as he lives with these *forms*; he reveals reality to himself, and himself to reality, in that he lets himself and the environment enter into this plastic medium, in which the two do not merely make contact, but fuse with each other.

Consequently all those theories which propose to find the roots of myth by exploring the realm of experience, of *objects*, which are supposed to have given rise to it, and from which it then allegedly grew and spread, must always remain one-sided and inadequate. There are, as is well known, a multitude of such explanations—a great variety of doctrines about the ultimate origin and real kernel of mythmaking, hardly less motley than the world of objects itself. Now it is found in certain psychical conditions and experiences, especially the phenomenon of dreaming, now in the contemplation of natural events, and among the latter it is further limited to the observation of natural objects such as the sun, the moon, the stars, or else to that of great occurrences such as storms, lightning and thunder, etc. Thus the attempt is made again and again to make soul mythology or nature mythology, sun or moon or thunder mythology the basis of mythology as such.

But even if one of these attempts should prove successful, this would not solve the real problem which mythology presents to philosophy, but at best would push it back one step. For mythical formulation as such cannot be understood and appreciated simply by determining the *object* on which it is immediately and originally centered. It is, and remains, the same miracle of the spirit and the same mystery, no matter whether it covers this or that realistic matter, whether it deals with the interpretation and articulation of psychical processes or physical things, and in the latter case, just what particular things these may be. Even though it were possible to resolve all mythology to a basic astral mythology—what the mythical consciousness derives from contemplation of the stars, what it *sees* in them directly, would still be something radically different from the view they present to empirical observation or the way they figure in theoretical speculation and scientific "explanations" of natural phenomena. Descartes said that theoretical science remains the same in its essence no matter what object it deals with—just as the sun's light is the same no matter what wealth and variety of things it may illuminate. The same may be said of any symbolic form, of language, art, or myth, in that each of these is a particular way of seeing, and carries within itself its particular and proper source of light. The function of envisagement, the dawn of a conceptual enlightenment can never be realistically derived from things themselves or understood through the nature of its objective contents. For it is not a question of what we see in a certain perspective, but of the perspective itself. If we conceive the problem in this way, it is certainly clear that a reduction of all myth to one subject matter brings us no nearer to the solution, in fact it removes us further than ever from any hope of a real answer. For now we see in language, art and mythology so many archetypal phenomena of human mentality which can be indicated as such, but

are not capable of any further "explanation" in terms
of something else. The realists always assume, as their
solid basis for all such explanations, the so-called "given,"
which is thought to have some definite form, some inherent structure of its own. They accept this reality as
an integrated whole of causes and effects, things and attributes, states and processes, of objects at rest and of
motions, and the only question for them is which of
these elements a particular mental product such as myth,
language or art originally embodied. If, for instance, the
phenomenon in question is language, their natural line
of inquiry must be whether names for things preceded
names for conditions or actions, or vice versa—whether,
in other words, nouns or verbs were the first "roots"
of speech. But this problem itself appears spurious as
soon as we realize that the distinctions which here are
taken for granted, the analysis of reality in terms of things
and processes, permanent and transitory aspects, objects
and actions, do not precede language as a substratum of
given fact, but that language itself is what initiates such
articulations, and develops them in its own sphere. Then
it turns out that language could not begin with any
phase of "noun concepts" or "verb concepts," but is the
very agency that produces the distinction between these
forms, that introduces the great spiritual "crisis" in
which the permanent is opposed to the transient, and
Being is made the contrary of Becoming. So the linguistic fundamental concepts must be realized as something prior to these distinctions, forms which lie between the sphere of noun conception and that of verb
conception, between thinghood and eventuality, in a
state of indifference, a peculiar balance of feeling.

A similar ambiguity seems to characterize the earliest

phases to which we can trace back the development of mythical and religious thought. It seems only natural to us that the world should present itself to our inspection and observation as a pattern of definite forms, each with its own perfectly determinate spatial limits that give it its specific individuality. If we see it as a whole, this whole nevertheless consists of clearly distinguishable units, which do not melt into each other, but preserve their identity that sets them definitely apart from the identity of all the others. But for the mythmaking consciousness these separate elements are not thus separately given, but have to be originally and gradually derived from the whole; the process of culling and sorting out individual forms has yet to be gone through. For this reason the mythic state of mind has been called the "complex" state, to distinguish it from our abstract analytic attitude. Preuss, who coined this expression, points out, for instance, that in the mythology of the Cora Indians, which he has studied exhaustively, the conception of the nocturnal heaven and the diurnal heaven must have preceded that of the sun, the moon, and the separate constellations. The first mythical impulse, he claims, was not toward making a sun-god or a lunar deity, but a community of stars. "The sun-god does indeed hold first rank in the hierarchy of the gods, but . . . the various astral deities can stand proxy for him. They precede him in time, he is created by them, by somebody's jumping into a fire or being thrown into it; his power is influenced by theirs, and he is artificially kept alive by feeding on the hearts of sacrificed victims, i.e., the stars. The starry night sky is the necessary condition for the existence of the sun; that is the central idea in the whole religious ideation of the Coras and of the ancient Mexicans, and must be regarded as a principal factor in the further development of their religion."[4]

The same function here attributed to the nocturnal heavens seems to be imputed by the Indo-Germanic races to the daylit sky. Their religions show many traces of the fact that the worship of light as an undifferentiated, total experience preceded that of the individual heavenly bodies, which figure only as its media, its particular manifestations. In the Avesta, for instance, Mithra is not a sun-god, as he is for later ages; he is the spirit of heavenly light. He appears on the mountaintops *before* the sun rises, to mount his chariot which, drawn by four white horses, runs the course of heaven during the day; when night comes, he the unsleeping still lights the face of earth with a vague glimmering light. We are explicitly told that he is neither the sun, nor the moon, nor any or all of the stars, but through them, his thousand ears and ten thousand eyes, he perceives everything and keeps watch over the world.[5]

Here we see in a concrete instance how mythic conception originally grasps only the great, fundamental, qualitative contrast of light and darkness, and how it treats them as *one* essence, one complex whole, out of which definite characters only gradually emerge. Like the spirit of language, the mythmaking genius "has" separate and individualized forms only in so far as it "posits" them, as it carves them out of the undifferentiated whole of its pristine vision.

This insight into the determining and discriminating function, which myth as well as language performs in

[4] Preuss, *Die Nayarit-Expedition I: Die Religion der Cora Indianer*, Leipzig, 1912. Cf. further, Preuss, *Die geistige Kultur der Naturvölker*, pp. 9 ff.

[5] Yasht X, 145; Yasna I, ii (35); cf. Cumont, *Textes et monuments figurés relatifs aux mystères de Mithra* (Brussels, 1899), I, p. 225.

the mental construction of our world of "things", seems to be all that a "philosophy of symbolic forms" can teach us. Philosophy as such can go no further; it cannot presume to present to us, *in concreto*, the great process of emergence, and to distinguish its phases for us. But if pure philosophy is necessarily restricted to a general, theoretical picture of such an evolution, it may be that philology and comparative mythology can fill in the outline and draw with firm, clear strokes what philosophical speculation could only suggestively sketch. An initial and portentous step in this direction has been taken by Usener in his work on divine names. "An Essay toward a Science of Religious Conception," is the subtitle he has given to his book, which brings it definitely into the realm of philosophical problems and systematic treatment. To trace the history of the divinities, their successive appearance and development among the several tribes of man, he tells us, is not an attainable goal; only a history of mythic ideas can be reconstructed. Such ideas, no matter how manifold, how varied, how heterogeneous they may appear at first sight, have their own inner lawfulness; they do not arise from a boundless caprice of the imagination, but move in definite avenues of feeling and creative thought. This intrinsic law is what mythology seeks to establish. Mythology is the science (λογος) of myth, or the science of the forms of religious conception.[6]

His findings in this field may certainly give pause to philosophers, who tend to regard the human mind as endowed *ab initio* with logical categories. "There have been long periods in mental evolution," he observes, "when the human mind was slowly laboring toward thought and conception and was following quite differ-

[6] Usener, *Götternamen. Versuch einer Lehre von der religiösen Begriffsbildung* (Bonn, 1896), p. 330; cf. esp. pp. v ff.

ent laws of ideation and speech. Our epistemology will not have any real foundation until philology and mythology have revealed the processes of involuntary and unconscious conception. The chasm between specific perception and general concepts is far greater than our academic notions, and a language which does our thinking for us, lead us to suppose. It is so great that I cannot imagine how it could have been bridged, had not language itself, without man's conscious awareness, prepared and induced the process. It is language that causes the multitude of casual, individual expressions to yield up one which extends its denotation over more and more special cases, until it comes to denote them all, and assumes the power of expressing a class concept" (p. 321).

Here, then, it is the philologist, the student of language and religion, who confronts philosophy with a new question, which emerges from his own investigations. And Usener has not merely indicated a new approach; he has resolutely followed it up, employing to this end all the clues which the history of language, the precise analysis of words, and especially that of divine names provided. The question naturally arises whether philosophy, not commanding any such materials, can handle this problem which the humanistic sciences have presented to it, and what intellectual resources it can tap to meet such a challenge. Is there any other line than the actual *history* of language and of religion that could lead us closer to the origin of primary linguistic and religious concepts? Or is it, at this point, one and the same thing to know the genesis of such ideas and to know their ultimate meanings and functions? This is the issue I propose to decide in the following pages. I shall take up Usener's problem in exactly the form in which he has cast it; but I shall attempt to tackle it on

the given name of a man, the conception of a *personality*. Thus a new Being has been produced, which continues to develop by a law of its own. The concept of the special god, which expressed a certain activity rather than a certain nature, now achieves its embodiment and appears, so to speak, in the flesh. This god is now capable of acting and suffering like a human creature; he engages in all sorts of actions, and instead of being wholly consummated in one function he is related to it as an independent subject. The many divine names which originally denoted a corresponding number of sharply distinguished special gods now fuse in one personality, which has thus emerged; they become the several appellations of this Being, expressing various aspects of his nature, power and range (pp. 301f., 325, 330).

What intrigues us about these results of Usener's, which we have tried to recapitulate in brief, is not primarily his material conclusion but the method by which he has arrived at it. That method is summed up in his preface with these words: "Only through devoted preoccupation with the spiritual traces of vanished times, that is to say, through philological research, can we train ourselves to feel with the past; then gradually sympathetic strains may be set in motion within us so that we find in our own consciousness the threads that link ancient and modern times. A greater wealth of observation and comparison allows us to go further and proceed from the particular case to a law. It would be a sad pass for human knowledge if detailed research *ipso facto* fettered the mind and prevented it from seeking a synoptic vision. The deeper you delve, the more you may expect to be rewarded by general insight."

Usener draws most of his material evidence from the history of Greek and Roman religion; yet he makes it perfectly clear that these demonstrations are merely representative instances of a pattern that is generally valid. Indeed, he specifically admits and stresses the fact that he gained his understanding of many important, basic traits in Graeco-Roman religion only through his extensive studies of Lithuanian paganism. And even in entirely unrelated fields, in American and African systems of belief, there are often astonishing parallels which serve to support and illuminate his fundamental theses in religious history and philosophy. In the detailed and careful account of the Evé tribe which Spieth has published there is a description of Evé gods that is nothing short of a paragon of what Usener has introduced under the name of "momentary deities."

"After the inhabitants of the town of Dzake in Peki had settled that place, a certain farmer at work in his fields went to look for water. In a trough-shaped hollow he drove his machete into the damp soil. Suddenly a gory looking stream welled up before him, of which he drank, and which he found refreshing. He told his family about it and persuaded them to come with him and worship that red fluid. After a while the water cleared, and all the family drank of it. From this time on, this water was a trō to its discoverer and to his kin. . . .

"It is said that upon the arrival of the first settlers of Anvlo a man happened to be standing before a great, thick breadfruit tree. At the sight of the tree, he felt panicky. He went to the priest to ask for an explanation of this event. The answer he received was that the tree was a trō which wanted to live with him and be worshipped by him. So his fright was the sign whereby the man knew that a trō had revealed itself to him. . . . If anyone takes refuge in an anthill from his human or animal persecutors, he will say afterwards: 'The anthill saved my life.' It is the same when a man finds safety in a brook from some raging wounded animal, or a family or entire clan takes shelter from the enemy in some mountain fastness. In every case the rescue is ascribed to some indwelling power of the object or place where, or by means of which, it occurred."[7]

The value of such observations for the general history of religions lies in the fact that here a dynamic concept of deity has taken the place of the static ones with which both are wont to operate; that the god or daemon is not merely described according to his nature and significance, but that the law of his origin is taken into consideration. An attempt is made to spy out his genesis from the mythico-religious consciousness, in fact to note the very hour of his birth. If empirical science, in the realms of etymology, religion and ethnology, finds itself faced with problems of this sort, surely no one can deny philosophy the right to essay them, and bring its own principles and interests to bear on their solution.

❧ 3 ❧

Language and Conception

TO know and understand the peculiar nature of mythico-religious conception not only through its results, but through the very principle of its formation, and to see,

[7] Spieth, *Die Religion der Eweer in Süd-Togo* (Leipzig, 1911), pp. 7f; cf. esp. Spieth's work on the Evé tribes (Berlin, 1906), pp. 462, 480, 490.—The examples here given are especially suited for refutation of Wundt's objection that Usener's "momentary gods" are "not really empirical data but rather logical postulates" (*Volkspsychologie*, IV, 561).

furthermore, how the growth of linguistic concepts is related to that of religious ideas and in what essential traits they coincide—this requires us, indeed, to reach far back into the past. We must not hesitate to take a roundabout way through general logic and epistemology, for it is only upon this basis that we may hope to determine precisely the *function* of this sort of ideation and to distinguish it clearly from the conceptual forms which serve theoretical thinking. According to the traditional teachings of logic, the mind forms concepts by taking a certain number of objects which have common properties, i.e., coincide in certain respects, together in thought and abstracting from their differences, so that only the similarities are retained and reflected upon, and in this way a general idea of such-and-such a class of objects is formed in consciousness. Thus the concept (*notio, conceptus*) is that idea which represents the totality of *essential* properties, i.e., the *essence* of the objects in question. In this apparently simple and obvious explanation, everything depends on what one means by a "property," and how such properties are supposed to be originally determined. The formulation of a general concept presupposes *definite* properties; only if there are fixed characteristics by virtue of which things may be recognized as similar or dissimilar, coinciding or not coinciding, is it possible to collect objects which resemble each other into a class. But—we cannot help asking at this point—how can such differentiae exist prior to language? Do we not, rather, *realize* them only by means of language, through the very act of naming them? And if the latter be the case, then by what rules and what criteria is this act carried out? What is it that leads or constrains language to collect just *these* ideas into a single whole and denote them by a word? What causes it to select, from the ever-flowing, ever-uniform stream of impressions which strike our senses or arise from the autonomous processes of the mind, certain pre-eminent forms, to dwell on them and endow them with a particular "significance"? As soon as we cast the problem in this mold, traditional logic offers no support to the student and philosopher of language; for its explanation of the origin of generic concepts presupposes the very thing we are seeking to understand and derive—the formulation of linguistic notions.[8] The problem becomes even more difficult, as well as more urgent, if one considers that the form of that ideational synthesis which leads to the primary verbal concepts and denotations is not simply and unequivocally determined by the object itself, but allows scope for the free operation of language and for its specific mental stamp. Of course, even this freedom must have its rules, and this original, creative power has a law of its own. Can this law be set forth, and can it be brought into relation with the principles that govern other spheres of spiritual expression, especially the rules of mythical, religious, and purely theoretical, i.e., scientific, conception?

Beginning with the last of these branches, we can show that all the intellectual labor whereby the mind forms general concepts out of specific impressions is directed toward breaking the isolation of the datum, wresting it from the "here and now" of its actual occurrence, relating it to other things and gathering it and them into some inclusive order, into the unity of a "system." The logical form of conception, from the standpoint of theoretical knowledge, is nothing but a preparation for the logical form of judgment; all judg-

[8] For more detailed discussion of this point see my *Philosophie der symbolischen Formen*, I, 244ff.

ment, however, aims at overcoming the illusion of singularity which adheres to every particular content of consciousness. The apparently singular fact becomes known, understood and conceptually grasped only in so far as it is "subsumed" under a general idea, recognized as a "case" of a law or as a member of a manifold or a series. In this sense every genuine judgment is synthetic; for what it intends and strives for is just this synthesis of parts into a whole, this weaving of particulars into a system. This synthesis cannot be achieved immediately and at a single stroke; it has to be worked out step by step, by a progressive activity of relating separate notions or sense impressions with each other, and then gathering up the resultant wholes into greater complexes, until finally the union of all these separate complexes yields the coherent picture of the totality of things. The will to this totality is the vivifying principle of our theoretical and empirical conception. This principle, therefore, is necessarily "discursive"; that is to say, it starts with a particular case, but instead of dwelling upon it, and resting content in sheer contemplation of the particular, it lets the mind merely start from this instance to run the whole gamut of Being in the special directions determined by the empirical concept. By this process of running through a realm of experience, i.e., of discursive thinking, the particular receives its fixed intellectual "meaning" and definite character. It has different appearances according to the ever-broadening contexts in which it is taken; the place it holds in the totality of Being, or rather the place which the progressive march of thought assigns to it, determines its content and its theoretical significance.

How this ideal of knowledge controls the rise of science, especially the construction of mathematical physics, requires no further elucidation. All the concepts of physics have no other aim than to transform the "rhapsody of perceptions," by which the world of sense is actually presented to us, into a system, a coherent epitome of laws. Each individual datum becomes a phenomenon and object of "nature" only as it meets this requirement—for "nature" in the theoretical sense, according to the Kantian definition, is nothing but the existence of things as determined by general laws.

A distinction has often been drawn between the "individualizing" mode of historical thought and the "generalizing" mode of science. While in the latter any concrete case is merely regarded as an instance of a general law, and while the "here" and "now" has no significance save in so far as it reveals a universal rule, it is said that history deliberately seeks out this here and now, in order to grasp it ever more precisely in just this character. But even in historical thinking the particular fact is significant only by virtue of the relationships into which it enters. Although it cannot be regarded as an instance of a general law, yet in order to be historically conceived, to appear *sub specie* the mode of history, it must take its place as a *member* of a course of events or belong to some teleological nexus. Its determination in time is the exact opposite of its temporal separateness; for historically it has meaning only if and as it refers back to a past and forward to a future. Thus all genuine historical reflection, instead of losing itself in contemplation of the *merely* singular and nonrecurrent, must strive, like the morphological thought of Goethe, to find those "pregnant" moments in the course of events where, as in focal points, whole series of occurrences are epitomized. In such points, phases of reality that are temporally widely separated become connected and linked for historical conception and understanding. As certain high moments are culled from the uniform stream of time, and are related to each other, and concatenated in series, the origin and end of all happenings, their whence and whither, is gradually illumined. So historical conception, too, is characterized by the fact that through it a thousand connections are forged by one stroke; and it is not so much the contemplation of particulars as an awareness of such relationships that constitutes the peculiar historicity, or what we call the historical significance of facts.

But let us not dwell longer on such general observations, because our concern is not primarily with the structure of scientific concepts; we are considering this structure only in order to clarify another, namely, the form and character of the primordial linguistic concepts. While this remains to be done, the purely logical theory of conception cannot be completely developed. For all the concepts of theoretical knowledge constitute merely an upper stratum of logic which is founded upon a lower stratum, that of the logic of language. Before the intellectual work of conceiving and understanding of phenomena can set in, the work of *naming* must have preceded it, and have reached a certain point of elaboration. For it is this process which transforms the world of sense impression, which animals also possess, into a mental world, a world of ideas and meanings. All theoretical cognition takes its departure from a world already preformed by language; the scientist, the historian, even the philosopher, lives with his objects only as language presents them to him. This immediate dependence is harder to realize than anything that the mind creates mediately, by conscious thought processes. It is easy to see that logical theory, which traces concepts back to an act of generalizing "abstraction," is of little use here; for this "abstraction" consists of selecting from the wealth of *given* properties certain ones which are common to several sensory or intuitive experiences; but our problem is not the choice of properties already given, but the *positing* of the properties themselves. It is to comprehend and illuminate the nature and direction of *noticing*, which must precede mentally the function of "denoting." Even those thinkers who have concerned themselves most actively with the problem of the "origin of language" have thought it necessary to stop at this point, and have simply assumed a "faculty" of the soul for the process of "noticing."

"When man attained that condition of reflection which is peculiar to him," says Herder in his essay on the origins of language, "and when this reflection first achieved free play, he invented speech." Suppose a certain animal, say a lamb, to pass before the eyes of a human being: what image, what view of it will present itself to him? Not the same that would arise for wolves or lions; they would smell and taste it mentally, be overcome by sensuality, and instinct would throw them upon it. Nor would man's image be like that of another animal to whom the lamb was of no direct interest; for such an animal would let it glide vaguely past, because its own instinct was turned in another direction. "But with man, not so! As soon as he is in a position to become acquainted with the lamb, there is no instinct to interfere with him; there is no sensuality to draw him into too close contact with it, or to repel him from it; it stands before him just as it meets his senses. White, gentle, woolly—his mind in its conscious exercise seeks a characteristic for it—the lamb bleats! He has found the differentia. His inner sense is activated. This bleating,

which has made the liveliest impression on his mind,
that freed itself from all other properties of sight and
touch, stood forth, and entered most deeply into his
experience—'Ah! You are the bleating one!'—remains
with him; he feels that he has recognized it *humanly*,
has interpreted it, in that he knows it by a property. . . .
By a property, then? And is that anything but by an
inward *denoting word*? The sound of bleating, thus apprehended by a human being as the character of the
sheep, became, through the medium of reflection, the
name of the sheep, even though his tongue had never
attempted to utter it."[9]

In these statements of Herder's one can still hear quite
clearly the echoes of those theories which he was com-
bating—the traces of the language theories of the Enlightenment, which derived language from conscious
reflection and considered it as something "invented."
Man looks for a differentia because he needs it; because
his reason, his specific faculty of "reflection" demands
it. This demand itself remains something underived—a
"basic power of the soul." Thus the explanation has
really progressed in a circle: for the end and goal of
language formation, the act of denotation by specific
properties, must be regarded as also the principle of its
beginning.

Humboldt's notion of the "inward form of language"
seems to lead in another direction. For he no longer
considers the "whence" of linguistic concepts, but is
concerned purely with their "what"; not their origin,
but the demonstration of their character constitutes his
problem. The form of observation, which underlies all
speech and language development, always expresses a
peculiar spiritual character, a special way of conceiving

[9] "Ueber den Ursprung der Sprache," *Werke* (ed. Supham), V, 35f.

and apprehending. The difference between the several languages, therefore, is not a matter of different sounds and marks, but of different world conceptions. If the moon is denoted in Greek as the Measuring One (μήν), in Latin as the Shining One (luna), or if even in one and the same language, as in Sanskrit, the elephant is called now the Twice Drinker, now the Two-Tusked One, now the Handed One—that goes to show that language never denotes simply objects, things as such, but always conceptions arising from the autonomous activity of the mind. The nature of concepts, therefore, depends on the way this active viewing is directed.

But even this notion of the inward form of language really has to presuppose that which it professes to prove and reveal. For, on the one hand, speech is here the vehicle of any world perspective, the medium through which thought must pass before it can find itself and assume a definite theoretical form; but, on the other hand, just this sort of form, this definite perspective has to be presupposed, in order to explain the particular character of any given language, its special way of seeing and denoting. So the question of the origin of language tends always to become—even for the thinkers who have taken it most profoundly and struggled hardest with it—a veritable monkey puzzle. All the energy devoted to it seems only to lead us about in a circle and finally leave us at the point from which we started.

And yet the very nature of such fundamental problems entails that the mind, though it despairs of ever finally solving them, can never quite let them alone. And we receive something like a new hope of a solution if, instead of comparing the primary linguistic forms with the forms of logical conception, we try to compare them with those of mythical ideation. What holds these

two kinds of conception, the linguistic and the mythical,
together in one category, and opposes both of them to
the form of logical thought, is the fact that they both
seem to reveal the same sort of intellectual apprehension, which runs counter to that of our theoretical
thought processes. The aim of theoretical thinking, as
we have seen, is primarily to deliver the contents of
sensory or intuitive experience from the isolation in
which they originally occur. It causes these contents to
transcend their narrow limits, combines them with
others, compares them, and concatenates them in a
definite order, in an all-inclusive context. It proceeds
"discursively," in that it treats the immediate content
only as a point of departure, from which it can run the
whole gamut of impressions in various directions, until
these impressions are fitted together into one unified
conception, one closed system. In this system there are
no more isolated points; all its members are reciprocally
related, refer to one another, illumine and explain each
other. Thus every separate event is ensnared, as it were,
by invisible threads of thought, that bind it to the
whole. The theoretical significance which it receives lies
in the fact that it is stamped with the character of this
totality.

Mythical thinking, when viewed in its most elementary forms, bears no such stamp; in fact, the character
of intellectual unity is directly hostile to its spirit. For
in this mode, thought does not dispose freely over the
data of intuition, in order to relate and compare them to
each other, but is captivated and enthralled by the intuition which suddenly confronts it. It comes to rest in
the immediate experience; the sensible present is so
great that everything else dwindles before it. For a person whose apprehension is under the spell of this

mythico-religious attitude, it is as though the whole world were simply annihilated; the immediate content, whatever it be, that commands his religious interest so completely fills his consciousness that nothing else can exist beside and apart from it. The ego is spending all its energy on this single object, lives in it, loses itself in it. Instead of a widening of intuitive experience, we find here its extreme limitation; instead of expansion that would lead through greater and greater spheres of being, we have here an impulse toward concentration; instead of extensive distribution, intensive compression. This focusing of all forces on a single point is the prerequisite for all mythical thinking and mythical formulation. When, on the one hand, the entire self is given up to a single impression, is "possessed" by it and, on the other hand, there is the utmost tension between the subject and its object, the outer world; when external reality is not merely viewed and contemplated, but overcomes a man in sheer immediacy, with emotions of fear or hope, terror or wish fulfillment: then the spark jumps somehow across, the tension finds release, as the subjective excitement becomes objectified, and confronts the mind as a god or a daemon.

Here we have the mythico-religious protophenomenon which Usener has sought to fix with the term "momentary god." "In absolute immediacy," he says, "the individual phenomenon is deified, without the intervention of even the most rudimentary class concept; that one thing which you see before you, that and nothing else is the god" (p. 280). To this day, the life of primitive races shows us certain features in which this process is almost tangibly clear. We may recall the examples of it which Spieth adduces: wafer found by a thirsty person, a termite mound that hides and saves someone, any new object that inspires a man with sudden terror—all these are transformed directly into gods. Spieth summarizes his observations with the words: "To the mind of the Evé, the moment in which an object or any striking attributes of it enter into any noticeable relation, pleasant or unpleasant, with the life and spirit of man, that moment a Trō is born in his consciousness." It is as though the isolated occurrence of an impression, its separation from the totality of ordinary, commonplace experience produced not only a tremendous intensification, but also the highest degree of *condensation*, and as though by virtue of this condensation the objective form of the god were created so that it veritably burst forth from the experience.

Now it is here, in this intuitive creative form of myth, and not in the formation of our discursive theoretical concepts, that we must look for the key which may unlock for us the secrets of the original conceptions of language. The formulation of language, too, should not be traced back to any sort of reflective contemplation, to the calm and clearheaded comparison of given sense impressions and the abstraction of definite attributes; but here again we must abandon this static point of view for the comprehension of the dynamic process which produces the verbal sound out of its own inner drive. To be sure, this retrospect in itself is not enough; for through it we are merely brought to the further, more difficult question, how it is possible for anything permanent to result from such a dynamism, and why the vague billowing and surging of sensory impressions and feelings should give rise to an objective, verbal "structure." The modern science of language, in its efforts to elucidate the "origin" of language, has indeed gone back frequently to Hamann's dictum, that poetry is "the

mother-tongue of humanity"; its scholars have emphasized the fact that speech is rooted not in the prosaic,
but in the poetic aspect of life, so that its ultimate basis
must be sought not in preoccupation with the objective
view of things and their classification according to certain attributes, but in the primitive power of subjective
feeling.[10] But although this doctrine may seem, at first
sight, to evade the vicious circle into which the theory
of logical expression is ever lapsing, in the end it also
cannot bridge the gulf between the purely denotative
and the expressive function of speech. In this theory, too,
there always remains a sort of hiatus between the lyrical
aspect of verbal expression and its logical character; what
remains obscure is exactly that *emancipation* whereby a
sound is transformed from an emotional utterance into
a denotative one.

Here we may be guided once more by consideration
of how the "momentary gods" were generated. If such a
god is, in his origin, the creation of a moment, if he
owes his existence to some entirely concrete and individual, never-recurring situation, he yet achieves a certain substantiality which lifts him far above this acci-
dental condition of his origin. Once he has been divorced
from the immediate exigency, the fear or hope of the
moment, he becomes an independent being, which
henceforth lives on by a law of its own, and has gained
form and continuity. He appears to men not as a creature
of the hour, but as an objective and superior power,
which they adore and which their cult endows with more
and more definite form. The image of the momentary
god, instead of merely preserving the memory of what
he originally meant and was—a deliverance from fear,

[10] See Otto Jespersen, *Progress in Language* (London, 1894), esp. pp.
332 ff.

the fulfillment of a wish and a hope—persists and remains long after that memory has faded and finally
disappeared altogether.

The same function which the image of the god performs, the same tendency to permanent existence, may
be ascribed to the uttered sounds of language. The
word, like a god or a daemon, confronts man not as a
creation of his own, but as something existent and significant in its own right, as an objective reality. As soon
as the spark has jumped across, as soon as the tension
and emotion of the moment has found its discharge in
the word or the mythical image, a sort of turning point
has occurred in human mentality: the inner excitement
which was a mere subjective state has vanished, and has
been resolved into the objective form of myth or of
speech. And now an ever-progressive objectification can
begin. In the same measure in which the autonomous
activity of man extends over a widening sphere, and becomes adjusted and organized within that sphere, his
mythical and verbal *world* undergoes a progressive organization and ever more definite articulation. The
"momentary gods" are succeeded by gods of activity, as
Usener has shown us through the examples of the Roman
"functional gods" and the corresponding Lithuanian
deities. Wissowa summarizes the basic character of
Roman religion with the words: "All their deities are
entirely practically conceived, so to speak—conceived as
being effective in those things with which the Roman
dealt in his ordinary life: the local environment in which
he moved, the various occupations in which he engaged,
the occasions that determine and shape the life of the
individual as well as the community—all these things
are in the keeping of clearly conceived gods with definitely recognized powers. For the Roman, even Jupiter

and Tellus were gods of the Roman community, gods of the hearth and the heath, of wood and wold, seedtime and harvest, of growth and flower and fruit."[11] Here one can trace directly how humanity really attains its insight into objective reality only through the medium of its own activity and the progressive differentiation of that activity; before man thinks in terms of logical concepts, he holds his experiences by means of clear, separate, mythical images. And here, too, the development of language appears to be the counterpart of the development which mythical intuition and thought undergo; for one cannot grasp the true nature and function of linguistic concepts if one regards them as copies, as representations of a definite world of facts, whose components are given to the human mind *ab initio* in stark and separate outlines. Again, the limits of things must first be posited, the outlines drawn, by the agency of language; and this is accomplished as man's activity becomes internally organized, and his conception of Being acquires a correspondingly clear and definite pattern.

We have already demonstrated that the primary function of linguistic concepts does not consist in the comparison of experiences and the selection of certain common attributes, but in the concentration of such experiences, so to speak, in distilling them down to one point. But the manner of this concentration always depends upon the direction of the subject's interest, and is determined not so much by the content of the experience as by the teleological perspective from which it is viewed. Whatever appears important for our wishing and willing, our hope and anxiety, for acting and doing: that and only that receives the stamp of verbal "meaning." Dis-

[11] G. Wissowa, *Religion und Kultus der Römer* (Munich, 1912), Vol. 2, pp. 24f.

tinctions in meaning are the prerequisite for that solidi-
fication of impressions which, as we said above, is a
necessary condition for their denotation by words. For
only what is related somehow to the focus point of willing
and doing, only what proves to be essential to the whole
scheme of life and activity, is selected from the uniform
flux of sense impressions, and is "noticed" in the midst
of them—that is to say, receives a special linguistic accent, a name. The beginnings of this process of "noticing" must undoubtedly be attributed even to animal
mentality; for in their world of experience, too, those
elements upon which their impulses and instincts center
are singled out by their conscious apprehension. Only
something that arouses a single impulse, such as the
nutritional or the sexual impulse, or anything that relates to it, "is there" for an animal as an objective content of its feeling and apperception. But such a presence
always fills just the actual moment in which the impulse
is evoked, is directly stimulated. As soon as the excitation abates, and the desire is fulfilled, the world of Being,
the order of perceptions collapses again. When a new
stimulus reaches the animal's consciousness, this world
may be resurrected; but it is always held in the narrow
confines of actual drives and excitations. Its successive
beginnings always fill just the present moment, without
ranging themselves in any progression; the past is but
dimly retained, the future does not become an image, a
prospect. Only symbolic expression can yield the possibility of prospect and retrospect, because it is only by
symbols that distinctions are not merely made, but fixed
in consciousness. What the mind has once created, what
has been culled from the total sphere of consciousness,
does not fade away again when the spoken word has set
its seal upon it and given it definite form.

Here, too, the recognition of function precedes that of Being. The aspects of Being are distinguished and co-ordinated according to a measure supplied by action—hence they are guided, not by any "objective" similarity among things, but by their appearance through the medium of practice, which relates them within a purposive nexus. This teleological character of verbal concepts may be readily supported and clarified by means of examples from the history of language.[12] A great many of the phenomena which philologists commonly treat under the general heading of "changes of meaning" can really be understood in principle only from this angle. If altered conditions of life, the changes that attend the advance of culture, have brought men into a new practical relation with their environment, the concepts inherent in language do not retain their original "sense." They begin to shift, to move about, in the same measure as the bounds of human activity tend to vary and efface each other. Wherever, for any reason, the distinction between two activities loses its importance and meaning, there is wont to be a corresponding shift of verbal meanings, namely, of the words which marked that distinction. A very characteristic instance of this sort of thing may be found in an article which Meinhof has published under the title, "On the Influence of Occupation on the Language of the Bantu Tribes in Africa." According to Meinhof, "The Herero have a word, *rima*, to denote sowing, which is phonetically identical with *lima*, the word for hoeing, cultivating, in other Bantu languages. The reason for this peculiar change of meaning is that the Herero neither sow nor cultivate the ground. They are cowherds, and their whole vocabulary

[12] In regard to the "teleological" structure of language, cf. the more detailed study in my *Philosophie d. symbolischen Formen*, I, 254ff.

smells of cows. Sowing and cultivating they deem un-
worthy occupations for a man; so they do not find it
worth while to draw nice distinctions among such in-
ferior tasks."[13]

Primitive languages especially furnish many further
examples in support of the principle that the order of
nomenclature does not rest on the external similarities
among things or events, but that different items bear the
same name, and are subsumed under the same concept,
whenever their *functional* significance is the same, i.e.,
whenever they hold the same place or at least analogous
places in the order of human activities and purposes.
Certain Indian tribes, for instance, are said to use the
same word for "dancing" and for "working"[14]—obviously
because the distinction between these two activities is
not immediately apparent to them, since in their scheme
of things dance and agriculture serve essentially the same
purpose of providing the means of livelihood. The
growth and prosperity of their crops seems to them to
depend as much or more on the correct performance of
their dances, their magical and religious ceremonies, than
on prompt and proper attention to the soil.[15] Such a
fusion of activities gives rise to the identification of their
respective names, the "concepts" of language. When
the natives along the Swan River in Africa were first introduced to the sacrament of Communion, they called
it a dance;[16] which goes further to show how a unity may

[13] "Ueber die Einwirkung der Beschäftigung auf die Sprache bei den
Bantustämmen Afrikas," *Globus*, Vol. 75 (1899), p. 361.

[14] "Die Tarahumara tanzen überhaupt nur zu Zauberzwecken bzw.
als 'Gebet.' Tanzen ist ihnen daher . . . gleich arbeiten, was aus der
Bedeutung des Wortes tanzen nolávoa hervorgeht." Preuss, "Der
Ursprung der Religion und Kunst," *Globus*, Vol. 87 (1905), p. 336.

[15] E. Reclus, *Le primitif d'Australie*, p. 28.

[16] Cf. Preuss, *Religion und Mythologie der Uitoto* (Göttingen and
Leipzig, 1923), I, 123ff.; II, 637f.

be posited by language in spite of all distinctions and even complete disparity of appearances, as long as the contents of experience agree in their functional import—in this case, their religious significance.[17]

Here is one of the basic motives by virtue of which mythical thinking transcends the original vagueness of "complex" intuitions and proceeds to concretely defined, distinctly sundered, and individualized mental constructions. This process, too, is determined primarily by the lines which activity takes; so much so that the forms of mythical invention reflect, not the objective character of *things*, but the forms of human practices. The primitive god, like primitive action, is limited to a very restricted sphere. Not only does every occupation have its particular god, but each phase of the total action becomes the domain of an independent god or daemon who governs this precise sphere of action. The Roman *Fratres Arvales*, when making atonement for the removal of trees from the sacred grove of the goddess Dia, divided the deed into a number of separate acts, for each of which a special deity was invoked: *Deferenda* for fetching down the wood, *Commolenda* for chopping it up, *Coinquenda* for splitting it, and *Adolenda* for burn-

[17] Here we may adduce a further striking example of this "teleological" construction of language, which I owe to a verbal communication from my colleague Professor Otto Dempwolff. In the Kâte language, which is current in New Guinea, there is a word *bilin*, which denotes a certain kind of grass with tough stems and roots that are wedged firmly in the soil; the latter are said to hold the earth together during earthquakes, so that it does not break apart. When nails were first introduced by Europeans, and when their use became popularly known, the natives applied this word to them—as also to wire and to iron rods, in short, to everything that served the purpose of holding things together.

Similarly, one may often observe in nursery language the creation of such teleological identities, which do not meet our class concepts at all, and seem even to defy them. Cf. Clara and William Stern, *Die Kindersprache* (Leipzig, 1906), pp. 26, 172, *et al.*

ing up the brushwood.[18] The same phenomenon may be
seen in primitive languages, which often divide an action
into several subactions, and instead of comprehending
it all under one term, denote each part by a separate
verb, as though they had to break up the idea into little
pieces in order to handle it. Perhaps it is not mere chance
that in the language of the Evé, who have such a wealth
of "momentary gods" and "special gods," this peculiarity
should be very pronounced.[19] And even where both
language and myth have risen considerably above such
momentary, sense-bound intuition, where they have
broken through their original fetters, they long remain
quite inseparably involved with each other. Their connection is, in fact, so close that it is impossible to determine on a basis of empirical data which of them takes
the lead in their progress toward universal formulation
and conception, and which one merely follows suit.
Usener, in a section of his work that is philosophically
one of the most significant parts, has sought to prove
that all general terms in language have had to go through
a certain mythical phase. The fact that in the Indo-
Germanic languages abstract concepts are usually denoted by feminine nouns, with the feminine ending -a
(-η), proves, according to Usener, that the idea this
feminine form expresses was originally not conceived as
an abstractum, but apprehended and felt as a female
deity.

"Can there be any doubt," he asks further, "whether
Φόβος came first, or φόβος, the divine image or the condition? Why should the condition be denoted as something of masculine gender, not as neuter, like τὸ δέος?
The first creation of the word must have been inspired

---

[18] Wissowa, *Religion und Kultus der Römer*, Vol. 2, p. 25.
[19] Westermann, *Grammatik der Ewe-Sprache* (Berlin, 1907), p. 95.

by some idea of a living, personal Being, the "Startler," the "Flight Producer"; in countless applications of the supposed abstract word, this Being still appears: εἰσῆλθεν or ἐνέπεσε Φόβος, the Startler stalks, or attacks, me! The same process must be assumed for the making of all feminized abstractions. The feminine adjective only became an abstraction after it had denoted a female personage, and in primitive times this could not have been conceived as anything but a goddess" (p. 375).

But does not the science of language as well as that of religion show signs of a converse process as well? Should we not suppose, for instance, that the way which inflected languages have of endowing every noun with a particular gender may have influenced the conceptions of mythico-religious imagination and bent them after its own fashion? Or may we deem it mere chance that among peoples whose language does not differentiate genders, but employs other and more complex principles of classification, the realm of myth and religion also exhibits an entirely different structure—that it represents all phases of existence not under the auspices of personal, divine powers, but orders it according to totemic groups and classes? We shall content ourselves with merely proposing this question, which would have to be answered by detailed scientific research. But whatever the verdict might be, it is evident that myth and language play similar roles in the evolution of thought from momentary experience to enduring conceptions, from sense impression to formulation, and that their respective functions are mutually conditioned. Together and in combination they prepare the soil for the great syntheses from which our mental creation, our unified vision of the cosmos springs.

≼§ 4 §≽

Word Magic

SO far we have sought to discover the common root of
linguistic and mythic conception; now arises the question, how this relationship is reflected in the structure
of the "world" that is given by speech and by myth.
Here we encounter a law that holds equally for all symbolic forms, and bears essentially on their evolution.
None of them arise initially as separate, independently
recognizable forms, but every one of them must first be
emancipated from the common matrix of myth. All
mental contents, no matter how truly they evince a
separate systematic realm and a "principle" of their
own, are actually known to us only as thus involved and
grounded. Theoretical, practical and aesthetic consciousness, the world of language and of morality, the basic
forms of the community and the state—they are all
originally tied up with mythico-religious conceptions.
This connection is so strong that where it begins to dissolve the whole intellectual world seems threatened with
disruption and collapse; so vital that as the separate forms
emerge from the original whole and henceforth show
specific characteristics against its undifferentiated background they seem to uproot themselves and lose some of
their own proper nature. Only gradually do they show
that this self-imposition is part of their self-development,
that the negation contains the embyro of a new assertion,
that the very divorcement becomes the starting point of
a new connection, which arises from extraneous postula-
tions.

The original bond between the linguistic and the

mythico-religious consciousness is primarily expressed in the fact that all verbal structures appear as *also* mythical entities, endowed with certain mythical powers, that the Word, in fact, becomes a sort of primary force, in which all being and doing originate. In all mythical cosmogonies, as far back as they can be traced, this supreme position of the Word is found. Among the texts which Preuss has collected among the Uitoto Indians there is one which he has adduced as a direct parallel to the opening passage of St. John, and which, in his translation, certainly seems to fall in with it perfectly: "In the beginning," it says, "the Word gave the Father his origin."[20] Of course, striking though it may be, no one would try to argue from this coincidence to any direct relationship or even an analogy of material content between that primitive creation story and the speculations of St. John. And yet it presents us with a certain problem, it points to the fact that some indirect relationship must obtain, which covers everything from the most primitive gropings of mythico-religious thought to those highest products in which such thought seems to have already gone over into a realm of pure speculation.

A more precise insight into the foundations of this relationship can be attained only in so far as we are able to carry back the study of those examples of Word veneration, which the history of religions is always uncovering, from the mere analogy of their respective *contents* to the recognition of their common *form*. There must be some particular, essentially unchanging *function* that endows the Word with this extraordinary, religious character, and exalts it *ab initio* to the religious sphere, the sphere of the "holy." In the creation accounts of almost all great cultural religions, the Word appears in

[20] Preuss, *Religion und Mythologie der Uitoto*, I, 25 f.; II, 659.

league with the highest Lord of creation; either as the
tool which he employs or actually as the primary source
from which he, like all other Being and order of Being,
is derived. Thought and its verbal utterance are usually
taken directly as one; for the mind that thinks and the
tongue that speaks belong essentially together. Thus, in
one of the earliest records of Egyptian theology, this
primary force of "the heart and the tongue" is attributed
to the creation-god Ptah, whereby he produces and
governs all gods and men, all animals, and all that lives.
Whatever is has come into being through the thought
of his heart and the command of his tongue; to these
two, all physical and spiritual being, the existence of the
Ka as well as all properties of things, owe their origin.
Here, as indeed certain scholars have pointed out, thousands of years before the Christian era, God is conceived
as a spiritual Being who *thought* the world before he
created it, and who used the Word as a means of expression and an instrument of creation.[21] And as all

[21] See Moret, *Mystères Egyptiens* (Paris, 1913), pp. 118ff., 138. Cf.
esp. Erman, "Ein Denkmal memphitischer Theologie," *Sitzungsbericht
der königlich-Preussischen Akademie der Wissenschaften*, XLIII
(1911), 916ff. An exact parallel to this may be found in a creation
hymn of Polynesia, which, according to Bastian's German translation
(here rendered into English), reads as follows:

> In the beginning, Space and the Companion,
> Space in the height of Heaven,
> Tananaoa filled; he ruled the Heaven,
> And Mutuhei wound himself above it.
> In those days was no voice, no sound,
> No living thing yet in motion.
> No day there was as yet, no light,
> Only a gloomy, black-dark night.
> Tananaoa it was who conquered the night,
> And Mutuhei's spirit the distance pierced.
> From Tananaoa Atea was sprung,
> Mighty, filled with the power of life,
> Atea it was, who now ruled the Day,
> And drove away Tananaoa."

"The basic idea is that Tananaoa induces the process in that the original physical and psychical Being rest in him, so do all ethical bonds and the whole moral order.

Those religions which base their world picture and their cosmogony essentially on a fundamental ethical contrast, the dualism of good and evil, venerate the spoken Word as the primary force by whose sole agency Chaos was transformed into an ethico-religious Cosmos. According to the Bundahish, the cosmogony and cosmography of the Parsis, the war between the power of Good and the power of Evil, i.e., between Ahura Mazda and Angra Mainyu, begins with Ahura Mazda's reciting the words of the Holy Prayer (Ahuna Vairya):

"He spake that which has twenty-one words. The end, which is his victory, the impotence of Angra Mainyu, the decline of the Daevas, the resurrection and the future life, the ending of opposition to the (good) creation for all eternity—all these he showed to Angra Mainyu . . . When a third of this prayer had been spoken, Angra Mainyu doubled up his body with terror, when two-thirds had been spoken he fell upon his knees, and when the whole had been uttered he was confounded, and powerless to abuse the creatures of Ahura Mazda, and remained confounded for three thousand years."[22]

Here, again the words of the prayer precede the material creation, and preserve it ever against the destructive powers of the Evil One. Similarly, in India, we find the

---

silence (Mutuhei) is removed through the production of Tone (Ono), and Atea (Light) is wedded with the Red Dawn (Atanua)." See Bastian, *Die heilige Sage der Polynesier, Kosmogonie u. Theologie* (Leipzig, 1881), pp. 13f; also Achelis, "Ueber Mythologie u. Kultus von Hawaii, *Das Ausland*, Vol. 66 (1893), p. 436.

[22] See *Der Bundehesh, zum ersten Male herausgegeben von Ferdinand Justi* (Leipzig, 1868), Chap. 1, p. 3.

power of the Spoken Word (Vāc) exalted even above the might of the gods themselves.

"On the Spoken Word all the gods depend, all beasts and men; in the Word live all creatures . . . the Word is the Imperishable, the firstborn of the eternal Law, the mother of the Veddas, the navel of the divine world."[23]

As the Word is first in origin, it is also supreme in power. Often it is the *name* of the deity, rather than the god himself, that seems to be the real source of efficacy.[24] Knowledge of the name gives him who knows it mastery even over the being and will of the god. Thus a familiar Egyptian legend tells how Isis, the great sorceress, craftily persuaded the sun-god Ra to disclose his name to her, and how through possession of the name she gained power over him and over all the other gods.[25] In many other ways, too, Egyptian religious life in all its phases evinces over and over again this belief in the supremacy of the name and the magic power that dwells

[23] *Taittiriya Brahm.*, 2, 8, 8, 4 (German by Gelder in his *Religionsgeschichtliches Lesebuch*, p. 125).

[24] According to the tradition of the Maori, upon their first immigration in New Zealand they did not take along their old gods, but only their mighty prayers, by means of which they were assured the power of bending the gods to their will. Cf. Brinton, *Religions of Primitive Peoples*, pp. 103f.

[25] "I am he," says Re in this story, "with many names and many shapes, and my form is in every god. . . . My father and my mother have told me my name, and it has remained hidden in my body since my birth, lest some sorcerer should acquire magic power over me thereby." Then said Isis to Re (who has been stung by a poisonous serpent of her creation, and is appealing to all the gods for help from the poison): "Tell me your name, father of gods, . . . that the poison may go out of you; for the man whose name is spoken, he lives." And the poison burned hotter than fire, so that the god could no longer resist. He said to Isis: "My name shall go forth from my body and over into thine." And he added: "Thou shalt conceal it, but to thy son Horus thou mayst reveal it as a potent spell against every poison." See Erman, *Aegypten u. aegyptisches Leben im Altertum*, II, 36off.; *Die aegyptische Religion*, Vol. 2, pp. 173f.

in it.[26] The ceremonies attending the anointment of kings are governed by minute prescriptions for the transference of the god's several names to the Pharaoh; each name conveys a special attribute, a new divine power.[27]

Moreover, this motive plays a decisive role in the Egyptian doctrines of the soul and its immortality. The souls of the departed, starting on their journey to the land of the dead, must be given not only their physical possessions, such as food and clothing, but also a certain outfit of a magical nature: this consists chiefly of the names of the gatekeepers in the nether world, for only the knowledge of these names can unlock the doors of Death's kingdom. Even the boat in which the dead man is conveyed, and its several parts, the rudder, the mast, etc., demand that he call them by their right names; only by virtue of this appellation can he render them willing and subservient and cause them to take him to his destination.[28]

The essential identity between the word and what it denotes becomes even more patently evident if we look at it not from the objective standpoint, but from a subjective angle. For even a person's ego, his very self and personality, is indissolubly linked, in mythic thinking,

[26] Cf. the examples cited by Budge, *Egyptian Magic* (London, 1911), Vol. 2, pp. 157ff.; also Hopfner, *Griechisch-Aegyptischer Offenbarungszauber* (Leipzig, 1921), pp. 680ff.

[27] Cf. esp. G. Foucart, *Histoire des religions et méthode comparative* (Paris, 1912), pp. 202f.: "Donner au Pharaon un 'nom' nouveau, dans lequel entrait la désignation d'un attribut ou d'une manifestation de l'Epervier, puis, plus tard, de Râ et l'ajouter aux autres noms du protocol royale, c'était pour les Égyptiens introduire dans la personne royale, et superposer aux autres éléments qui la composaient déjà, un être nouveau, exceptionnel, qui était une incarnation de Râ. Ou, plus exactement, c'était bel et bien détacher de Râ une des vibrations, une des âmes forces, dont chacune est lui tout entier; et en la faisant entrer dans la personne du Roi, c'était transformer toute celle-ci en un nouvel exemplaire, un nouveau support matériel de la divinité."

[28] For further details see Budge, *op. cit.*, pp. 164ff.

with his name. Here the name is never a mere symbol,
but is part of the personal property of its bearer; property which must be carefully protected, and the use of
which is exclusively and jealously reserved to him. Sometimes it is not only his name, but also some other verbal
denotation, that is thus treated as a physical possession,
and as such may be acquired and usurped by someone
else. Georg von der Gabelentz, in his book on the science
of language, mentions the edict of a Chinese emperor of
the third century B.C., whereby a pronoun in the first
person, that had been legitimately in popular use, was
henceforth reserved to him alone.[29] And the name may
even acquire a status above the more or less accessory
one of a personal possession, when it is taken as a truly
substantial Being, an integral *part* of its bearer. As such
it is in the same category as his body or his soul. It is
said of the Eskimos that for them man consists of three
elements—body, soul, and name.[30] And in Egypt, too,
we find a similar conception, for there the physical body
of man was thought to be accompanied, on the one
hand, by his Ka, or double, and, on the other, by his
name, as a sort of spiritual double. And of all these three
elements it is just the last-mentioned which becomes
more and more the expression of a man's "self," of his
"personality."[31] Even in far more advanced cultures this
connection between name and personality continues to
be felt. When, in Roman law, the concept of the "legal
person" was formally articulated, and this status was denied to certain physical subjects, those subjects were
also denied official possession of a proper name. Under

[29] *Die Sprachwissenschaft*, p. 228.
[30] See Brinton, *Religions of Primitive Peoples*, p. 93.
[31] Cf. Budge, *op. cit.*, p. 157; also Moret, *Mystères Egyptiens*,
p. 119.

Roman law a slave had no legal name, because he could not function as a legal person.[32]

In other ways, too, the unity and uniqueness of the name is not only a mark of the unity and uniqueness of the person, but actually constitutes it; the name is what first makes man an individual. Where this verbal distinctiveness is not found, there the outlines of his personality tend also to be effaced. Among the Algonquins, a man who bears the same name as some given person is regarded as the latter's other self, his alter ego.[33] If, in accordance with a prevalent custom, a child is given the name of his grandfather, this expresses the belief that the grandfather is resurrected, reincarnated in the boy. As soon as a child is born, the problem arises which one of his departed ancestors is reborn in him; only after this has been determined by the priest can the ceremony be performed whereby the infant receives that progenitor's name.[34]

Furthermore, the mythic consciousness does not see human personality as something fixed and unchanging, but conceives every *phase* of a man's life as a new personality, a new self; and this metamorphosis is first of all made manifest in the changes which his name undergoes. At puberty a boy receives a new name, because, by virtue of the magical rites accompanying his initiation, he has ceased to exist as a boy, and has been reborn as a

[32] Mommsen, *Römisches Staatsrecht*, III, 1, p. 203; cf. Rudolph Hirzel, "Der Name—ein Beitrag zu seiner Geschichte im Altertum u. besonders bei den Griechen," *Abhandlungen der sächsischen Gesellschaft der Wissenschaften*, Vol. XXVI (1918), p. 10.

[33] "The expression in the Algonkin tongue for a person of the same name is *nind owiawina*, 'He is another myself.'" (Cuoq, *Lexique Algonquine*, p. 113, quoted from Brinton, *op. cit.*, p. 93). Cf. esp. Giesebrecht, *Die alttestamentliche Schätzung des Gottesnamens in ihrer religionsgeschichtlichen Grundlage* (Königsberg, 1901), p. 89.

[34] See, for instance, Spieth, *Die Religion der Eweer*, p. 229.

man, the reincarnation of one of his ancestors.[35] In other
cases the change of name sometimes serves to protect a
man against impending danger; he escapes by taking on
a different self, whose form makes him unrecognizable.
Among the Evé it is customary to give children, and
especially those whose elder brothers or sisters have died
young, a name that has a frightful connotation, or attributes some non-human nature to them; the idea is
that Death may be either frightened away, or deceived,
and will pass them by as though they were not human
at all.[36] Similarly, the name of a man laboring under disease or bloodguilt is sometimes changed, on the same
principle, that Death may not find him. Even in Greek
culture this custom of altering names, with its mythic
motivation, still maintained itself.[37] Quite generally, in
fact, the being and life of a person is so intimately connected with his name that, as long as the name is pre-
served and spoken, its bearer is still felt to be present and
directly active. The dead may, at any moment, be literally "invoked," the moment those who survive him speak
his name. As everyone knows, the fear of such visitation
has led many savages to avoid not only every mention
of the departed, whose name is tabooed, but even the
enunciation of all assonances to his name. Often, for
instance, an animal species whose name a defunct person
had borne has to be given a different appellation, lest
the dead man be inadvertently called upon by speaking

[35] Characteristic examples may be found especially among the initia-
tion rites of Australian native tribes; cf. esp. Howitt, *The Native
Tribes of South East Australia* (London, 1904), and James, *Primitive
Ritual and Belief* (London, 1917), pp. 16 ff.

[36] Cf. Spieth, *op. cit.*, p. 230.

[37] Hermippos 26, 7:

διὰ τοῦτο καλῶς ἡμῖν θεῖοι καὶ ἱεροὶ ἄνδρες ἐθέσπισαν ἐναλλάττειν τὰ τῶν
ἀποιχομένων ὀνόματα, ὅπως τελωνοῦντας αὐτοὺς κατὰ τὸν ἐναέριον τόπον
λανθάνειν ἐξῇ καὶ διέρχεσθαι.

of the beast.[38] In many cases procedures of this sort, entirely mythic in their motivation, have had a radical influence on language, and modified vocabularies considerably.[39] And the further a Being's power extends, the more mythic potency and "significance" he embodies, the greater is the sphere of influence of his name. The rule of secrecy, therefore, applies first and foremost to the Holy Name; for the mention of it would immediately release all the powers inherent in the god himself.[40]

Here, again, we are faced with one of the prime and essential motives which, rooted as it is in the deepest layers of mythical thought and feeling, maintains itself even in the highest religious formulations. Giesebrecht has traced the origin, extent and development of this motive throughout the Old Testament, in his work, *Die alttestamentliche Schätzung des Gottesnamens und ihre religionsgeschichtliche Grundlage*. But early Christianity, too, still labored entirely under the spell of this idea.

"The fact that the name functions as proxy for its bearer," says Dieterich in his *Eine Mithrasliturgie*, "and to speak the name may be equal to calling a person into being; that a name is feared because it is a real power;

[38] Ten Kate, "Notes ethnographiques sur les Comanches," *Revue d'Ethnographie*, IV, 131 (cited from Preuss, "Ursprung der Religion u. Kunst," *Globus*, Vol. 87, p. 395).

[39] Name taboos, I am told in a personal communication from Meinhof, play a vital part especially in Africa; among many Bantu tribes, for instance, women are not allowed to speak the names of their husbands or their fathers, so they are compelled to invent new words.

[40] For later Greek magical practices, cf. Hopfner, *Griechisch-ägyptischer Offenbarungszauber*, § 701, p. 179: "Je höher und mächtiger der Gott war, desto kräftiger und wirksamer musste auch sein wahrer Name sein. Daher ist es ganz folgerichtig anzunehmen, dass der wahre Name des einen Urgotts, des Schöpfers ($\delta\eta\mu\iota\upsilon\rho\gamma\acute{o}s$) für Menschen überhaupt unerträglich sei: denn dieser Name war ja zugleich auch das Göttliche an sich und zwar in seiner höchsten Potenz, daher für die schwache Natur des Sterblichen viel zu stark; daher tötet er den, der ihn hört."

that knowledge of it is sought because being able to speak it bestows control of that power on the knower—all these facts indicate clearly what the early Christians were still feeling and trying to express when they said 'In God's name' instead of 'In God,' or 'In Christ's name' for 'In Christ.' . . . Thus we can understand such expressions as βαπτίζειν εἰς τὸ ὄνομα Χριστοῦ instead of βαπτίζειν εἰς Χριστόν; the name is pronounced over the font, and thereby takes possession of the water and pervades it, so that the neophyte is quite literally immersed in the name of the Lord. The congregation, whose liturgy begins with the words: 'In the name of God,' was thought at the time to be within the bourne of the name's efficacy (no matter how figuratively and formally the phrase is taken). 'Where two or three are gathered together in my name, (εἰς τὸ ἐμὸν ὄνομα) there am I in the midst of them' (Matthew 18:20) means simply, 'Where they pronounce my name in their assembly, there I am really present.' Ἁγιασθήτω τὸ ὄνομά σου once had a much more concrete sense than one would ever suspect from the hermeneutics of the several churches and their doctrines."[41]

The "special god," too, lives and acts only in the particular domain to which his name assigns and holds him. Whoever, therefore, would be assured of his protection and aid must be sure to enter his realm, i.e., to call him by his "right" name. This need explains the phraseology of prayer, and of religious speech in general, both in Greece and in Rome—all the turns of phrase which ring a change on the several names of the god, in order to obviate the danger of missing the proper and essential appellation. Concerning the Greeks, this practice is recorded for us by a well-known passage in Plato's *Kraty-*

los;[42] in Rome it produced a standing formula, in which the various terms of invocation, corresponding to the several aspects of the god's nature and will, are disjoined by "either — or," "sive — sive."[43] This stereotyped mode of address must be repeated every time; for every act of devotion to the god, every appeal directed to him, commands his attention only if he is invoked by his appropriate name. The art of right address, therefore, was developed in Rome to the point of a sacerdotal technique, which produced the *indigitamenta* in the keeping of the pontifices.[44]

But here let us stop; for it is not our intention to collect theological or ethnological material, but to clarify and define the problem presented by such material. Such interweaving and interlocking as we have found between the elements of language, and the various forms of religious and mythical conception cannot be due to mere chance; it must be rooted in a common characteristic of language and myth as such. Some scholars have sought to base this intimate connection on the suggestive power of words, and especially of a spoken command, to which primitive man is supposed to be particularly subject; the magical and daemonic power which all verbal utterance has for the mythic state of consciousness seems to them to be nothing more than an objectification of that experience. But such a narrow empirical and pragmatic foundation, such a detail of personal or social experience, cannot support the prime and fundamental facts of linguistic and mythic conception. More and more clearly we see ourselves faced with the question whether the close

[42] Plato, *Kratylos*, 400E.
[43] For details see Norden, *Agnostos Theos: Untersuchungen zur Formengeschichte religiöser Rede* (Leipzig, 1913), pp. 143 ff.
[44] Cf. Wissowa, *Religion und Kultus der Römer*, Vol. 2, p. 37.

relationship of contents which certainly obtains between
language and myth may not be most readily explained
by the common form of their evolution, by the conditions which govern both verbal expression and mythic
imagination from their earliest, unconscious beginnings.
We have found these conditions given by a type of apprehension that is contrary to theoretical, discursive
thinking. For, as the latter tends toward expansion, im-
plication and systematic connection, the former tends
toward concentration, telescoping, separate characterization. In discursive thought, the particular phenomenon
is related to the whole pattern of being and of process;
with ever-tightening, ever more elaborate bonds it is held
to that totality. In mythic conception, however, things
are not taken for what they mean indirectly, but for their
immediate appearance; they are taken as pure presenta-
tions, and embodied in the imagination. It is easy to see
that this sort of hypostatization must lead to an entirely
different attitude toward the spoken word, toward its
power and content, than the standpoint of discursive
thought would produce. For theoretical thinking, a word
is essentially a vehicle serving the fundamental aim of
such ideation: the establishment of relationships between the given phenomenon and others which are
"like" it or otherwise connected with it according to
some co-ordinating law. The significance of discursive
thought lies entirely in this function. In this sense, it is
something essentially ideal, a "sign" or symbol, the object of which is not a substantial entity but lies rather in
the relations it establishes. The word stands, so to speak,
between actual particular impressions, as a phenomenon
of a different order, a new intellectual dimension; and
to this mediating position, this remoteness from the
sphere of immediate data, it owes the freedom and ease

with which it moves among specific objects and connects one with another.

This free ideality, which is the core of its *logical* nature, is necessarily lacking in the realm of mythic conception. For in this realm nothing has any significance or being save what is given in tangible reality. Here is no "reference" and "meaning"; every content of consciousness to which the mind is directed is immediately translated into terms of actual presence and effectiveness. Here thought does not confront its data in an attitude of free contemplation, seeking to understand their structure and their systematic connections, and analyzing them according to their parts and functions, but is simply captivated by a total impression. Such thinking does not develop the given content of experience; it does not reach backward or forward from that vantage point to find "causes" and "effects," but rests content with taking in the sheer existent. When Kant defined "reality" as any content of empirical intuition which follows general laws and thus takes its place in the "context of experience," he gave an exhaustive definition of the concept of reality in the canons of discursive thought. But mythic ideation and primitive verbal conception recognize no such "context of experience." Their function, as we have seen, is rather a process of almost violent separation and individuation. Only when this intense individuation has been consummated, when the immediate intuition has been focused and, one might say, reduced to a single point, does the mythic or linguistic form emerge, and the word or the momentary god is created. And this peculiar genesis determines the type of intellectual content that is common to language and myth; for where the process of apprehension aims not at an expansion, extension, universalizing of the content, but

rather at its highest intensification, this fact cannot fail
to influence human consciousness. All other things are
lost to a mind thus enthralled; all bridges between the
concrete datum and the systematized totality of experience are broken; only the present reality, as mythic or
linguistic conception stresses and shapes it, fills the entire subjective realm. So this one content of experience
must reign over practically the whole experiential world.
There is nothing beside or beyond it whereby it could be
measured or to which it could be compared; its mere
presence is the sum of all Being. At this point, the word
which denotes that thought content is not a mere conventional symbol, but is merged with its object in an
indissoluble unity. The conscious experience is not
merely wedded to the word, but is consumed by it.
Whatever has been fixed by a name, henceforth is not
only real, but is Reality. The potential between "symbol"
and "meaning" is resolved; in place of a more or less
adequate "expression," we find a relation of identity, of
complete congruence between "image" and "object,"
between the name and the thing.

From another angle, too, we may observe and elucidate this substantial embodiment which the spoken
word undergoes: for the same sort of hypostatization or
transubstantiation occurs in other realms of mental
creativity; indeed, it seems to be the typical process in
all unconscious ideation. All cultural work, be it technical or purely intellectual, proceeds by the gradual shift
from the direct relation between man and his environment to an indirect relation. In the beginning, sensual
impulse is followed immediately by its gratification; but
gradually more and more mediating terms intervene
between the will and its object. It is as though the will,
in order to gain its end, had to move away from the

goal instead of toward it; instead of a simple reaction, almost in the nature of a reflex, to bring the object into reach, it requires a differentiation of behavior, covering a wider class of objects, so that finally the sum total of all these acts, by the use of various "means," may realize the desired end.

In the realm of technical achievement this increasing mediation may be seen in the invention and use of tools. But here, again, it may be observed that as soon as man employs a tool, he views it not as a mere artifact of which he is the recognized maker, but as a Being in its own right, endowed with powers of its own. Instead of being governed by his will, it becomes a god or daemon on whose will he depends—to which he feels himself subjected, and which he adores with the rites of a religious cult. Especially the ax and the hammer seem to have attained such religious significance in earliest times;[45] but the cult of other implements, too, such as the hoe or the fishhook, the spear or the sword, may be found to this day among primitive peoples. Among the Evé the smith's hammer (Zu) is deemed a mighty deity whom they worship and to whom they make sacrifices.[46] And even in Greek religion and Greek classical literature the sentiment that prompts such a cult often finds direct expression. As an example of this, Usener has drawn attention to a passage in the Seven against Thebes of Aeschylos, in which Parthenopaeus swears by his spear, which he "honors above god, and above his eyes," to destroy Thebes. "Life and Victory depend upon direction and power, as also on the good will of the weapon; this feeling wells up irresistibly in the crucial moment of the

[45] Examples of this may be found, e.g., in Beth's Einführung in die vergleichende Religionsgeschichte (Leipzig, 1920), pp. 24ff.

[46] Spieth, Religion der Eweer, p. 115.

battle; and prayer does not invoke a god from afar to guide the weapon—the weapon itself is god, the helper and deliverer."[47]

An implement, then, is never regarded as something simply manufactured, something thought of and produced, but as a "gift from above." Its origin does not go back to man himself, but to some "culture hero," either a god or an animal. This attribution of all cultural values to a "savior" is so universal that attempts have been made to find the essence and origin of the god concept in this notion.[48] Again we are faced with a characteristic of mythic thinking which divides it sharply from the way of "discursive," or theoretical, reflection. The latter is characterized by the fact that even in apparently immediately "given" data it recognizes an element of mental creation, and stresses this active ingredient. Even in matters of fact it reveals an aspect of mental formulation; even in sheer sense data it traces the influence of a "spontaneity of thought" that goes to their making.— But while logical reflection tends, in this wise, to resolve all receptivity into spontaneity, mythic conception shows exactly the opposite tendency, namely, to regard all spontaneous action as receptive, and all human achievement as something merely bestowed. This holds for all the technical means of culture, and no less for its intellectual tools. For between these two sorts of implement there is originally no sharp dividing line, but rather a fluid distinction. Even purely mental assets and achievements, such as the words of human speech, are at first conceived entirely in the category of physical existence and the physical support of mankind. Preuss

---

[47] Usener, *Götternamen*, p. 285.
[48] Cf. Kurt Breysig, *Die Entstehung des Gottesgedankens u. der Heilbringer*, Berlin, 1905.

reports that, according to the Cora Indians and the Uitoto, the "Patriarch" created men and nature, but that since this creation he no longer interferes directly with the course of events. In lieu of such personal intervention, he gave to men his "Words," i.e., his cult and the religious ceremonies by means of which they now control nature and attain whatever is necessary for the welfare and perpetuation of the race. Without these holy spells which were originally given into their keeping, men would be entirely helpless, for nature yields nothing merely in return for human labor.[49] Among the Cherokees, too, it is an accepted belief that success in hunting or fishing is due chiefly to the use of certain words, of the proper magic formulas.[50]

It was a long evolutionary course which the human mind had to traverse, to pass from the belief in a physico-magical power comprised in the Word to a realization of its spiritual power. Indeed, it is the Word, it is language, that really reveals to man that world which is closer to him than any world of natural objects and touches his weal and woe more directly than physical nature. For it is language that makes his existence in a community possible; and only in society, in relation to a "Thee," can his subjectivity assert itself as a "Me." But here again the creative act, while it is in progress, is not recognized as such; all the energy of that spiritual achievement is projected into the result of it, and seems bound up in that object from which it seems to emanate as by reflection. Here, too, as in the case of tools and

[49] For details see Preuss, *Die Nayarit-Expedition*, I, LXVIIIf.; *Religion u. Mythologie der Uitoto* I, 25f; cf. also Preuss's article: "Die höchste Gottheit bei den kulturarmen Völkern," *Psychol. Forschungen*, II, 1922.

[50] Cf. Mooney, "Sacred Formulas of the Cherokee," *VIIth Annual Report of the Bureau of Ethnology* (Smithsonian Institution).

instruments, all spontaneity is felt as receptivity, all creativity as being, and every product of subjectivity as so much substantiality. And yet, this very hypostatization of the Word is of crucial importance in the development of human mentality. For it is the first form in which the spiritual power inherent in language can be apprehended at all; the Word has to be conceived in the mythic mode, as a substantive being and power, before it can be comprehended as an ideal instrument, an organon of the mind, and as a fundamental function in the construction and development of spiritual reality.

⇜§ 5 §⇝

The Successive Phases of Religious Thought

ACCORDING to Usener, the lowest level to which we can trace back the origin of religious concepts is that of "momentary gods," as he calls those images which are born from the need or the specific feeling of a critical moment, sprung from the excitation of mythico-religious fantasy, and still bearing the mark of all its pristine volatility and freedom. But it appears that the new findings which ethnology and comparative religion have put at our disposal during the three decades since the publication of Usener's work enable us to go back one step further yet. A few years before Usener's book there appeared a work by the English missionary Codrington: *The Melanesians: Studies in their Anthropology and Folk-Lore* (1891), which enriched the discipline of religious history by a very important concept. Codrington shows the root of all Melanesian religion to be the concept of a "supernatural power," which permeates all things and events, and may be present now in objects, now in persons, yet is never bound exclusively to any single and individual subject or object as its host, but may be transmitted from place to place, from thing to thing, from person to person. In this light, the whole existence of things and the activity of mankind seem to be embedded, so to speak, in a mythical "field of force," an atmosphere of potency which permeates everything, and which may appear in concentrated form in certain extraordinary objects, removed from the realm of everyday affairs, or in specially endowed persons, such as distinguished warriors, priests, or magicians. The core of this world view, however, of the "mana" concept which Codrington found among the Melanesians, is not so much the idea of such particular embodiments, as the notion of a "power" in general, able to appear now in this form, now in that, to enter into one object and then into another; a power that is venerated for its "holiness" as well as feared for the dangers it contains. For that power which is conceived in a positive sense as "mana" has also a negative aspect as the power of "taboo." Every manifestation of the divine potency, be it vested in persons or things, animate or inanimate, falls outside the realm of the "profane," and belongs to a special sphere of being which has to be separated from the ordinary and mundane by set lines of division, and by all sorts of protective measures.

Since Codrington's early discoveries, the science of ethnology has proceeded to trace the diffusion of these concepts all over the earth. Certain terms that correspond exactly to the meaning of mana may be found not only among the South Sea Islanders, but also among a great many American Indian tribes, as well as in Australia and in Africa. Precisely the same notion of a universal, essentially undifferentiated Power may be found in the Algonquin "manitu," the "wakanda" of the Sioux, the "orenda" of the Iroquois, and in various African religions. On the basis of such observations, students of ethnology and comparative religion have largely come to regard this conception not merely as a universal phenomenon, but as nothing less than a special category of mythic consciousness. The "Taboo-Mana Formula" has been regarded as the "minimum definition of religion," i.e., as the expression of a distinction which constitutes one of the essential, indispensable conditions of religious life as such, and represents the lowest level of it that we know.[51]

Concerning the proper interpretation of this formula, and of the mana concept and its various equivalents, ethnologists have, indeed, reached no general agreement. In fact, their several renderings and attempted explanations still stand in complete variance to one another. "Preanimistic" theories alternate with "animistic" ones; interpretations which treat the mana as something material are opposed to others which stress its dynamic nature and tend to regard it purely as a force.[52] But this very disagreement may serve to bring us closer to the actual sense of the mana conception; for it demonstrates

[51] Cf. especially Marett, "The Taboo-mana Formula as a minimum Definition of Religion," *Archiv für Religionswissenschaft*, XII (1909), and "The Conception of Mana," *Transactions of the 3rd Internat. Congress for the Hist. of Religion* (Oxford, 1908), I (reprinted in *The Threshold of Religion*, London, 1909, 3rd ed. 1914, pp. 99ff). See also Hewitt, "Orenda and a Definition of Religion," *American Anthropologist*, N.S. IV (1902), pp. 36ff.

[52] An excellent critical survey of the various theories represented in ethnological literature may be found in F. R. Lehmann's work, *Mana; der Begriff des "Ausserordentlich Wirkungsvollen" bei Südseevölkern*, Leipzig, 1922.

the fact that this conception is still quite indifferent, one might say "neutral," to a host of distinctions which our theoretical view of being and happening and our advanced religious feeling would apply to it. A survey of the available material tends rather to show that this indifference is an essential trait of the mana conception, and that the more one tries to "determine" it, i.e., to interpret it in the categories of distinctions and contradictions familiar to our thinking, the more widely one misses its true nature. Codrington himself attempted the first and most obvious characterization of it when he described it as not only a supernatural and magical power, but a mental or "spiritual" power as well. But the problematical aspect of this characterization appeared even in his own examples of it. For they show clearly that the content and compass of the mana idea do not coincide at all with our idea of the "spiritual"—whether the latter be conceived as something of *personal* character, or merely as determined by an *animate*, as opposed to inanimate, nature.[53] For not everything animate, nor everything spiritual possesses mana, but only that which, for one reason or another, is endowed with heightened, extraordinary effective powers; and moreover, mana may belong to mere things, if they exhibit some rare form that excites the mythic imagination, and thereby rise above the realm of everyday experience. It appears, therefore, that the idea of mana and the various conceptions related to it are not bound to a particular realm of *objects* (animate or inanimate, physical or spiritual), but that they should rather be said to indicate a certain "character," which may be attributed to the most diverse objects and

[53] Hewitt demonstrates, through a detailed linguistic comparison, that the orenda of the Iroquois, too, is not equivalent to their notions of either spiritual forces or merely life forces, but is a conception and expression *sui generis* (*op. cit.*, p. 44 ff.).

events, if only these evoke mythic "wonder" and stand forth from the ordinary background of familiar, mundane existence. As Söderblom says, in summarizing the results of his exhaustive and exact analysis of the concept: "The words in question [mana, manitu, orenda, etc.] have ambivalent meaning and are variously translated as remarkable, very strong, very great, very old, strong in magic, wise in magic, supernatural, divine— or in a substantive sense as power, magic, sorcery, fortune, success, godhead, delight."[54]

Such meanings, utterly disparate to our logical sense, can yield some sort of unity only if this unity be sought in a certain type not of content, but of mental attitude, of conception. It is not a matter of "what," but of "how"; not the object of attention, but the sort of attention directed to it, is the crucial factor here. Mana and its several equivalents do not denote a single, definite predicate; but in all of them we find a peculiar and consistent *form of predication*. This predication may indeed be designated as the primeval mythico-religious predication, since it expresses the spiritual "crisis" whereby the holy is divided from the profane, and set apart from the sphere of the ordinary, in a religious sense indifferent, reality. By this process of division the object of religious experience may really be said to be brought into existence, and the realm in which it moves to be first established. And herewith we have arrived at the crucial factor for our general problem: for our original aim was to treat both language and myth as spiritual functions which do not take their departure from a world of given objects, divided according to fixed and finished "attributes," but which actually first produce this organization of reality

[54] Söderblom, *Das Werden des Gottesglaubens; Untersuchungen über die Anfänge der Religion* (German ed., Leipzig, 1916), p. 95.

and make the positing of attributes possible. The concept of mana and the correlative, negative concept of taboo reveal the ways in which this construction is originally effected.

From the fact that we are here moving on a level where the mythic and religious world has not yet attained any fixed form, but is presented to us, so to speak, *in statu nascendi*, we may gain insight into the many-colored, variegated play of meanings in the word—and the concept—of mana. It is quite telling that even the attempt to determine the word class to which it belongs seems to encounter difficulties at every turn. According to our habits of thinking and speaking, the easiest way is to take it simply as a noun. This makes mana a sort of substance, which represents the quintessence of all the magic powers contained in individual things. It creates a unified existent thing, which may, however, distribute itself over various beings or objects. And since, moreover, this unity was conceived not only as existent, but as animate and personified, the concept of mana was endowed with our own basic notion of "spirit"—witness the way one has often interpreted the manitu of the Algonquins and the wakanda of the Sioux as nothing but their respective designations of the "Great Spirit," which, one naturally assumed, they adored as the creator of the world.

But a more precise analysis of the words and their meanings has nowhere borne out this interpretation. It showed that quite apart from any category of *personal* being, which is never really strictly applicable, even the mere concept of a thing with independent, substantial existence is too rigid to render the fleeting, elusive idea that is here to be grasped. Thus McGee observed, concerning the wakanda of the Sioux, that the reports of missionaries, according to which it expressed the concept of a personal, original being, were completely discredited by more scholarly language studies. "Among these tribes the creation and control of the world and the things thereof are ascribed to 'wa-ka^n-da' (the term varying somewhat from tribe to tribe), just as among the Algonquin tribes omnipotence was ascribed to 'ma-ni-do' ('Manito the Mighty' of 'Hiawatha'); yet inquiry shows that waka^{n}da assumes various forms, and is rather a quality than a definite entity. Thus among many of the tribes the sun is waka^{n}da—not *the* waka^{n}da or a waka^{n}da, but simply waka^{n}da; and among the same tribes the moon is waka^{n}da, and so is thunder, lightning, the stars, the winds, the cedar, and various other things; even a man, especially a shaman, might be waka^{n}da or a waka^{n}da. In addition the term was applied to mythic monsters of the earth, air, and waters; and according to some of the sages the ground or earth, the mythic underworld, the ideal upperworld, darkness, etc., were waka^{n}da or waka^{n}das. So, too, the fetiches and the ceremonial objects and decorations. . . . In like manner many natural objects and places of striking character were considered waka^{n}da. Thus the term was applied to all sorts of entities and ideas, and was used (with or without inflectional variations) indiscriminately as substantive and adjective, and with slight modification as verb and adverb. Manifestly a term so protean is not susceptible of translation into the more highly differentiated language of civilization. Manifestly, too, the idea expressed by the term is indefinite, and cannot justly be rendered into 'spirit,' much less 'Great Spirit'; though it is easy to understand how the superficial inquirer, dominated by definite spiritual concept(s), handicapped by unfamiliarity with the Indian tongue, misled by ignorance of the vague prescriptorial ideation, and perhaps deceived by crafty native informants or mischievous interpreters, came to adopt and perpetuate the erroneous interpretation. The term may be translated into 'mystery' perhaps more satisfactorily than into any other single English word, yet this rendering is at the same time much too limited and much too definite. As used by the Siouan Indian, waka^{n}da vaguely connotes also 'power,' 'sacred,' 'ancient,' 'grandeur,' 'animate,' 'immortal,' and other words, yet does not express with any degree of fullness and clearness the ideas conveyed by these terms singly or collectively—indeed, no English sentence of reasonable length can do justice to the aboriginal idea expressed by the term waka^{n}da."[55]

According to the findings of ethnologists and philologists, much the same thing is true of the Divine Name in the Bantu languages, and of the fundamental intuition it embodies. These tongues offer a special criterion whereby we may evaluate the conception in question; for the Bantu languages divide all nouns into different classes, and as they draw a sharp distinction between personal and impersonal nouns, the subsumption of the Divine Name under one of these heads allows us to infer immediately the character it denotes. And as a matter of fact the word *mulungu*, which our missionaries have accepted as the equivalent of our word "God," is assigned in the East Bantu dialect, for instance, to the impersonal class of nouns, to which its prefix and other formal characteristics assimilate it. Of course, this fact in itself still allows of other interpretation; it is possible to view such linguistic properties as signs of degeneration, indicating a regress of religious consciousness.

[55] McGee, "The Siouan Indians," 15th *annual report of the Bureau of Ethnology* (Smithsonian Institution), pp. 128f.

Roehl, for instance, says in his grammar of the Shambala language:

"The conception of God as a personal being has been practically lost among the Shambalas; they speak of God as of an impersonal spirit, inherent in all nature. The *Mulungu* lives in the bush, in separate trees, in cliffs, in caves, in wild animals (lions, snakes, cats), in birds, in locusts, etc. For such a *Mulungu* there is no possible place in class I (the personal class)."[56]

An exactly opposite interpretation has been given by Meinhof, who summarizes the results of a painstaking analysis of the mulungu concept in the light of religious and linguistic studies, to the effect that the word denotes primarily the *place* of ancestral spirits and, secondly, the *power* which emanates from that spot. "But this power remains something ghostly; it is not personified, and accordingly is not treated grammatically as a personal entity, except where a foreign religion has introduced a heightened conception of its nature."[57] Examples of this

[56] Roehl, *Versuch einer systematischen Grammatik der Schambala-sprache* (Hamburg, 1911), pp. 45ff. Another characteristic report on the "impersonal" nature of the mulungu concept is contained in Hetherwick's account of its use among the Yao of British Central Africa: "In its native use and form the word [mulungu] does not imply personality, for it does not belong to the personal class of nouns. . . . Its form denotes rather a state or property inhering in something, as the life or health inheres in body. Among the various tribes where the word is in use as we have described, the missionaries have adopted it as the word for 'God.' But the untaught Yao refuses to assign to it any idea of being a personality. It is to him more a quality or faculty of the human nature whose signification he has extended so as to embrace the whole spirit world. Once after I have endeavored to impress an old Yao headman with the personality of the Godhead in the Christian sense of the term, using the term *Mulungu*, my listener began to talk of 'Che Mulungu,' 'Mr. God,' showing that originally to him the word conveyed no idea of the personality I was ascribing to it." Hetherwick, "Some animistic beliefs among the Yaos of British Central Africa," *Journal of the Anthropol. Inst. of Great Britain and Ireland*, XXXII (1902), p. 94.

[57] Meinhof, "Die Gottesvorstellung bei den Bantu," *Allgemeine Missions-Zeitschrift*, Vol. 50 (1923), p. 69.

sort are instructive for us especially because they show us that the level of mythic conception on which we find ourselves here corresponds to a level of linguistic conception to which we may not assign offhand our grammatical categories, our neat classifications of sharply distinguished words. If we would have a verbal analogue to the mythic conceptions here at issue, we must, apparently, go back to the most primitive level of *interjections*.[58] The manitu of the Algonquins, the mulungu of the Bantus is used in this way—as an exclamation which indicates not so much a thing as a certain *impression*, and which is used to greet anything unusual, wonderful, marvelous or terrifying.[59]

At this point one can see how far prior the level of consciousness which begets these verbal forms is even to that on which the "momentary gods" are produced. For the momentary god, despite his transiency, is nevertheless always an individual, personal form, whereas here the holy, the divine, that which besets a man with sudden terror or wonder, still has an entirely impersonal, one might say "anonymous," character. But this nameless Presence forms the background against which definite daemonic or divine images can take shape. If the "mo-

[58] In a few cases this connection may still be traced even etymologically. Thus Brinton derives the wakanda of the Sioux from an interjection of wonder and amazement (*Religions of Primitive Peoples*, p. 60).

[59] According to a report by Roger Williams, cited by Söderblom (*op. cit.*, p. 100), it is customary among the Algonquins, when they note anything unusual in men, women, birds, beasts, or fish, to exclaim: *Manitu!* that is: "This is a god!" When therefore, they converse with each other of English ships and great buildings, of plowing the fields, and especially of books and letters, they end with: "*Mannitowok*," "Those are gods," "*Cummannitowok*," "You are a god." Compare especially Hetherwick, *op. cit.*, p. 94: "Mulungu is regarded as the agent in anything mysterious. It's mulungu, is the Yao exclamation on being shown anything that is beyond the range of his understanding. The rainbow is always 'mulungu' although some Yaos have begun to use the Mang' anya term 'uta wa Lesa,' 'bow of Lesa.'"

mentary god" is the first *actual* form originated by the creative, mythico-religious consciousness, this actuality is grounded, none the less, in the general potency of mythico-religious feeling.[60] The division of the realm of the "holy" from that of the "profane" is the prerequisite for any *definite* divinities whatsoever. The Self feels steeped, as it were, in a mythico-religious atmosphere, which ever enfolds it, and in which it now lives and moves; it takes only a spark, a touch, to create the god or daemon out of this charged atmosphere. The outlines of such daemonic beings may be ever so vague—yet they indicate the first step in a new direction.[61]

At this point, mythic thinking veers from its original, "anonymous" stage to the exact opposite, the phase of "polynomy." Every deity unites in itself a wealth of attributes, which originally belonged to the special gods that have all been combined in one new god. Their successor, however, inherits not only all their attributes, but also their names—not as his proper name, but as appellatives; for the name and nature of the god are the same thing. Thus the polynomy of the personal deities is an essential trait in their very being. "For religious feeling,

[60] This expression of "potency" has been involuntarily adopted by those who have sought to describe the mana conception and its related notions; cf., e.g., Hewitt's definition (op. cit., p. 38): "Orenda is a hypothetic potency or potentiality to do or effect results mystically." Cf. also Hartland's Presidential Address in the *Report of the British Association for the Advancement of Science*, York, 1906, pp. 678 ff.

[61] Again, symptoms of this "indeterminateness" may be found in language, in the ways such daemonic natures are frequently denoted; for instance, in the Bantu dialects the names of such beings do not have the prefix of the first class, which comprises names of "independent agents, persons"; there is, instead, a separate prefix, which, according to Meinhof, is used for spirits, in so far as they are regarded "not as independent personalities, but as that which animates or befalls persons; thus they apply to sicknesses, as also to smoke, fire, streams, or the moon, as natural powers." (Meinhof, *Grundzüge einer vergleichenden Grammatik der Bantusprachen*, Berlin, 1906, pp. 6f. Cf. note 59.)

the power of a god is expressed in the abundance of his epithets; polynomy is a prerequisite for a god of the higher, personal order."[62] In the Egyptian writings, Isis appears as the thousand-named, the ten-thousand-named, the myrionyma;[63] in the Koran, Allah's might finds expression in his "hundred names." In the native American religions, too, and especially the Mexican, this wealth of divine names is illustrated.[64]

So it may be said that the concept of godhead really receives its first concrete development and richness through language. As it emerges into the bright light of speech, it ceases thereby to be a mere outline and a shade. But a contrary impulse, too, inherent in the nature of language, is awakened anew in this process: for as speech has a tendency to divide, determine and fixate, so it has also, no less strongly, a tendency to generalize. So, guided by language, the mythic mind finally reaches a point where it is no longer contented with the variety, abundance and concrete fullness of divine attributes and names, but where it seeks to attain, through the unity of the word, the unity of the God-idea. But even here man's mind does not rest content; beyond this unity, it strives for a concept of Being that is unlimited by any particular manifestation, and therefore not expressible in any word, not called by any name.

[62] Usener, *Götternamen*, p. 334.

[63] Cf. Brugsch, *Religion u. Mythologie der alten Aegypter*, Leipzig, 1888, p. 645; for the expression "Isis Myrionyma," which is found also in Latin inscriptions, see Wissowa, *Religion und Kultus der Römer*, Vol. 2, p. 91.—In magical practice, this concept of the "polynomy" of gods has become regular stock in trade; thus we find, in Graeco-Egyptian magic formulas and prayers, invocations of Dionysius and Apollo in which the several names whereby they are called are arranged in alphabetical order, so that each verse presents a letter of the alphabet. For details see Hopfner, *Griechisch-Aegyptischer Offenbarungszauber*, Sec. 684, p. 175.

[64] For details see Brinton, *Religions of Primitive Peoples*, p. 99.

Here the cycle of mythico-religious thinking is completed. But the beginning and the end do not resemble each other; for we have progressed from a realm of mere indeterminateness to the realm of true generality. The Divine, instead of entering into the welter of properties and proper names, the gay kaleidoscope of phenomena, is set off against this world as something without attributes. For every mere "attribute" would limit its pure essence; *omnis determinatio est negatio.* It is especially the cult of mysticism, in all ages and among all peoples, that grapples again and again with this intellectual double problem—the task of comprehending the Divine in its totality, in its highest inward reality, and yet avoiding any particularity of name or image. Thus all mysticism is directed toward a world beyond language, a world of silence. As Meister Eckhardt has written, God is "the simple ground, the still desert, the simple silence" (der einveltige grunt, die stille wueste, die einveltic stille"); for "that is his nature, that he is one nature."[65]

The spiritual depth and power of language is strikingly evinced in the fact that it is speech itself which prepares the way for that last step whereby it is itself transcended. This most difficult and peculiar achievement is represented by two fundamental, linguistically grounded concepts—the concept of "Being," and the concept of the "Ego." Both appear to belong, in their complete significance, to a relatively late development of language; both show, in their grammatical forms, clear traces of the difficulties which verbal expression encountered in face of these concepts, and could master only by slow degrees. In regard to the concept of Being, a glance at the development and the original etymological meaning

[65] See Fr. Pfeiffer, *Deutsche Mystiker des vierzehnten Jahrhunderts,* Vol. II: *Meister Eckhardt* (Leipzig, 1857), p. 160.

of the *copula* in most languages shows how verbally oriented thinking arrived only very gradually at a distinction between "being" and "being-so." The "is" of the copula almost unfailingly goes back to a sensuously concrete original meaning; instead of conveying mere existence or a general state of being, it originally denoted a particular kind and form of appearance; especially being in a certain place, at a specific point in space.[66]

Now, when the growth of language achieves the liberation of the concept of Being from its bondage to some specific *form* of existence, it thereby furnishes mythico-religious thought with a new vehicle, a new intellectual tool. Critical, or "discursive," thinking, it is true, finally progresses to a point at which the expression of "being" appears as the expression of a *relation*, so that, to speak with Kant, Being is no longer a "possible predicate of a thing," and therefore can no longer be an attribute of God. But for mythic thought, which recognizes no such critical distinction, but remains "substantive" even in its highest reaches, Being is not only a predicate, but at a certain stage of development actually becomes the Predicate of Predicates; it becomes the expression which allows one to subsume all the attributes of God under a single rubric. Wherever, in the history of religious thought, the demand for the Unity of the Deity arises, it takes its stand on the linguistic expression of Being, and finds its surest support in the Word. Even in Greek philosophy this course of religious thinking may still be traced; even in Xenophanes we find the Unity of God derived and proved from the Unity of Being. But this connection is by no means restricted to philosophical speculation; it goes back to the oldest known records in

[66] Illustrations of this principle may be found in my *Philosophie der symbolischen Formen*, Vol. I, pp. 287 ff.

the history of religion. In early Egyptian texts, in the
midst of all the gods and animals of the Egyptian pantheon, we encounter the idea of the "hidden God," who
is referred to in the inscriptions as the One whose form
no one has known, whose image no one has discovered;
"He is a secret to his creation," "His name is a secret
to his children." There is but one designation that may
be applied to him, besides that of Creator, Maker of
men and gods: that is the designation of pure Being. He
begets and is not begotten, he bears and is not born,
he is Being, the Constant in everything, the Remaining
in all. Thus he "Is from the beginning," "Is from the
first"; everything that is, became after he was.[67] Here
all separate, concrete and individual divine names have
been resolved into the one name of Being; the Divine
excludes from itself all particular attributes, it cannot be
described through anything else, but can be predicated
only of itself.

From here it is but a single step to the fundamental
idea of true monotheism. This step is accomplished as
soon as the unity which so far has been sought through
the objective world, and expressed in objective terms,
is turned into a subjective essence, and the meaning of
divinity is approached not through the existence of
things, but through the being of the Person, the Self.
What has been said about the expression of "Being"
may also be said about the denotation of the "I"—it had
to be gradually found in the course of language making,
and had to be derived, slowly and stepwise, from concrete, purely sensory beginnings. But as soon as the
expression "I" is finally coined, religious thought has
gained a new category. And again it is religious language

[67] Compare the excerpts and translations from inscriptions, in Brugsch,
Religion und Mythologie der alten Aegypter, pp. 56ff., 96ff.

that seizes upon the new expression, and uses it, as it were, for a rung to reach a new spiritual height. The form of "self-predication," of self-revelation of the god through a constantly reiterated "I am . . . ," which reveals the various aspects of his unified being, originates in Egypt and Babylon; afterward, in later stages, it develops into a typical stylistic form of religious expression.[68] But its final form is not met with until it excludes all other forms; where, accordingly, the only "name" for the god is the name of the Self. When God, revealing himself to Moses, is asked what name Moses should bear to the Israelites, in case they want to know what god has sent him to them, the answer is: "I am that I am. Thus thou shalt say to them: I am has sent me unto you." It is only by this transformation of objective existence into subjective being that the Deity is really elevated to the "absolute" realm, to a state that cannot be expressed through any analogy with things or names of things. The only instruments of speech that remain for its expression are the personal pronouns: "I am he; I am the first, the last," as it is written in the Prophetic Books.[69]

Finally, both lines of contemplation—that which uses the notion of Being, and that which uses the notion of Self—are gathered up into one, in the speculations of India. This philosophy, too, takes its departure from the "Holy Word," the Brahma. In the Vedic books it is the power of this Holy Word to which all Being, even the gods, must submit. The Word rules and guides the course of nature; knowledge and possession of it gives the initiate

[68] For the origin and dissemination of this form see the exhaustive studies by Norden (instructive also for students of religious philosophy): *Agnostos Theos*, pp. 177 ff., 207 ff.

[69] Isaiah 48: 12; cf. 43: 10. For the significance of the "I am he," see Goldziher, *Der Mythos bei den Hebräern* (Leipzig, 1876), pp. 359 ff.

power over everything in the world. At first, it is treated entirely as a particular, to which some particular phase of existence is subject; in its use, the priest has to observe the most meticulous detail—any deviation by even a syllable, any change in rhythm or meter would void the potency of the prayer. But the progress from the Vedas to the Upanishads shows us how the Word is gradually liberated from this magic circle, and becomes an all-inclusive intellectual potency. From the essences of particular things, expressed in their separate concrete denotations, human thought rises to the unity that encompasses them all. The power of individual words is distilled, so to speak, into the power of the Word as such, the Brahma.[70] In this, all particular being, everything that seems to have a "nature" of its own, is represented; but by virtue of this inclusion it is at once divested of its "nature." In order to express this relationship, religious speculation is driven again to the concept of Being, which the Upanishads, seeking to grasp its abstract meaning, now present in a sort of heightened form, a higher potential. As Plato contrasted the ὄντα, the world of empirical things, with the ὄντως ὄν, the pure Being of the Idea, so we find in the Upanishads the world of particular existence opposed to the Brahma as the "Being-in-Being" ("satyasya satyam").[71]

This development presently meets and interpenetrates

[70] For the fundamental meaning of Brahma as the "Holy Word," as prayer and incantation, cf. Oldenberg, in the *Anzeiger für indogermanische Sprach= und Altertumskunde*, Vol. VIII, p. 40; also Oldenberg, *Die Religion der Upanishaden und die Anfänge des Buddhismus* (Göttingen 1915), pp. 17 ff., 38 ff., 46 ff. A somewhat divergent explanation is given by Hopkins, who regards the concept of power as the fundamental notion of Brahma, and believes this concept to have been transferred later to the word as prayer, with its magical potency. (Hopkins, *Origin and Evolution of Religion*, New Haven, 1923, p. 309.)

[71] Examples may be found in Deussen, *Philosophie der Upanishads* (Leipzig, 1899), pp. 119 ff.

with the other, which takes its departure from the opposite pole: the intellectual progression which treats not Being but Self as the keynote of religious thought. Both converge on the same goal; for Being and Self, Brahma and Atman, are distinct only in expression, not in content. The Self is the only thing that neither ages nor passes, that is unchangeable and immortal, and therefore is the true "Absolute." But by taking this final step, by identifying Brahma and Atman, religious thought and speculation has again broken its original bounds, the bounds of language. For words can no longer grasp and hold this unity of "subject" and "object." Language now vacillates *between* subjective and objective, it moves ever from one to the other, from the second back to the first; but this means that even in combining the two it always has to recognize them as separate ideas. When religious speculation denies this distinction, it claims independence from the power of the word and the guidance of language; but thereby it arrives at the transcendental, which is inaccessible not only to language, but to conception as well. The only name, the only denotation that remains for this Pan-Unity is the expression of negation. Being is Atman, who is called "No, no"; above this "It is not so" there is nothing further, nothing higher. So this revolt of the mind, which severs the bond between language and mythico-religious thought, only goes to demonstrate once more how strong and close is this bond; for as myth and religion seek to transcend the bourne of language, they arrive therewith at the limits of their own creative and formulative power.

When, in the year 1878, Max Müller published his *Lectures on the Origin and Growth of Religion,* he leaned heavily on the first reports he received by letter from Codrington concerning the mana of the Melane-

sians, which he used in support of his fundamental
thesis in philosophy of religion—the thesis that all religion is grounded in the power of the human mind to
grasp the "Infinite." "What I hold," he says, "is that
with every finite perception there is a concomitant perception, or, if that word should seem too strong, a concomitant sentiment or presentiment of the infinite; that
from the very first act of touch, or hearing, or sight, we
are brought in contact, not only with a visible, but at the
same time with an invisible universe."

And in the word "mana," which he interpreted as "a
Polynesian name for the Infinite," he saw one of the
earliest and clumsiest expressions of what Man's conception of the Infinite may have been in its most primitive stages.[72]

Our increasing acquaintance with the mythico-religious
realm to which the conception and expression "mana"
belongs has completely destroyed the nimbus of in-
finity and supersensoriness which surrounded the word,
as Müller understood it; it has shown us how thoroughly
the "religion" of mana is grounded not only in sense
perception, but in sensual desires, in absolutely "finite"
practical interests.[73] Indeed, Müller's interpretation is
possible only because he equated the "infinite" with the
"indefinite," the "interminable" with the "indeterminate."[74] But the fluidity of the mana concept, which
makes it so hard for us to grasp, or to find any verbal

[72] See Friedrich Max Müller, *Lectures on the Origin and Growth of
Religion* (New impression, London, 1898), pp. 46ff.

[73] "All Melanesian religion," says Müller, citing a letter of Codrington's, "in fact, consists in getting this Mana for oneself, or getting it
used for one's benefit—all religion, that is, as far as religious practices
go, prayers and sacrifices."

[74] "What I want to prove in this course of lectures is that indefinite
and infinite are in reality two names for the same thing" (*op. cit.*,
p. 36).

equivalent for it in our language pattern, has nothing whatever to do with the philosophical or religious idea of the Infinite. As the latter is *above* the possibility of exact verbal determination, so the former is still *below* such fixation. Language moves in the middle kingdom between the "indefinite" and the "infinite"; it transforms the indeterminate into a determinate idea, and then holds it within the sphere of finite determinations. So there are, in the realm of mythic and religious conception, "ineffables" of different order, one of which represents the lower limit of verbal expression, the other the upper limit; but between these bounds, which are drawn by the very nature of verbal expression, language can move with perfect freedom, and exhibit all the wealth and concrete exemplification of its creative power.

Here, again, the mythmaking mind exhibits a sort of consciousness of the relationship between its product and the phenomenon of language, though characteristically it can express this relationship not in abstract logical terms, but only in images. It transforms the spiritual dawn which takes place with the advent of language into an objective fact, and presents it as a cosmogonic process. Jean Paul remarks somewhere: "It seems to me that, just as animals drift through the outer world as though it were a dark undulating sea, so man, too, would be lost in the starry vastness of external perceptions, could he not divide that vague brightness into constellations by the agency of language, and thus resolve the whole into its parts for his consciousness." This emergence from the vague fullness of existence into a world of clear, verbally determinable forms, is represented in the mythic mode, in the imagist fashion peculiar to it, as the opposition between chaos and creation. And again it is speech that makes the transition from the featureless matrix of Being to its form and organization. Thus the Babylonian-Assyrian myth of creation describes Chaos as the condition of the world when the heavens above were "unnamed" and on earth no name was known for any thing. In Egypt, too, the time before creation is called the time when no god existed and no name for any object was known.[75]

From this indefinite state arises the first determinate existence when the creator god utters his own name, and by virtue of the power dwelling in that word calls himself into being. The idea that this god is his own cause, a real *causa sui*, is mythically expressed in the story of his origin through the magical force of his name. Before him there was no god, nor was any god beside him, "there was for him no mother who made his name for him, nor father who uttered it, saying: 'I have begotten him.' "[76] In the Book of the Dead, the sun-god Râ is represented as his own creator in that he gives himself his names, i.e., his characters and his powers.[77] And from this original power of speech which dwells in the demiurge arises everything else that has existence and definite being; when he speaks, he causes the birth of gods and men.[78]

The same motif occurs, with a somewhat different turn and a new depth of meaning, in the Biblical account of

[75] A. Moret, *Le Rituel du culte divin journalier en Egypte* (Paris, 1902), p. 129.

[76] From a Leyden papyrus. See A. Moret, *Mystères Egyptiens*, pp. 120 f.

[77] *Book of the Dead* (ed. Naville), 17, 6; cf. Erman, *Die aegyptische Religion* (Berlin, 1909), p. 34.

[78] Compare this passage with the examples given by Moret in the section "le mystère du verbe créateur" of his *Mystères Egyptiens*, pp. 103ff.; also Lepsius, "*Aelteste Texte des Totenbuches*, p. 29. How this Egyptian notion of the creative power of the word was combined with the fundamental ideas and concepts of Greek philosophy, and what this combination has meant to the development of the Christian Logos-idea, has been set forth by Reitzenstein in his *Zwei religionsgeschichtliche Fragen* (Strassburg, 1901), esp. pp. 80 ff.

Creation. Here, too, it is the word of God that separates light from darkness and produces the heavens and the earth. But the names of earthly creatures are no longer directly given by the Creator, but have to wait their assignment by Man. After God has created all the beasts of the field and the fowls of the air he brings them to man, to see what he will call them. "And whatsoever Adam called every living creature, that was the name thereof." (Genesis 2: 19). In this act of appellation, man takes possession of the world both physically and intellectually—subjects it to his knowledge and his rule. This special feature reveals that fundamental character and spiritual achievement of pure monotheism of which Goethe remarked that it is always uplifting because the belief in the one and only God makes man aware of his own inner unity. This unity, however, cannot be discovered except as it reveals itself in outward form by virtue of the concrete structures of language and myth, in which it is embodied, and from which it is afterward regained by the process of logical reflection.

⋙ 6 ⋘

The Power of Metaphor

THE foregoing considerations have shown us how mythical and verbal thought are interwoven in every way; how the great structures of the mythic and linguistic realms, respectively, are determined and guided through long periods of their development by the same spiritual motives. Yet one fundamental motive has so

far remained unnoticed, which not only illustrates their
relationship, but offers an ultimate explanation of it.
That myth and language are subject to the same, or at
least closely analogous, laws of evolution can really be
seen and understood only in so far as we can uncover
the common root from which both of them spring. The
resemblances in their results, in the forms which they
produce, point to a final community of function, of the
principles whereby they operate. In order to recognize
this function and represent it in its abstract nakedness,
we have to pursue the ways of myth and language not
in their progress, but in regress—back to the point from
which those two divergent lines emanate. And this common center really seems to be demonstrable; for, no matter how widely the contents of myth and language may
differ, yet the same form of mental conception is opera-
tive in both. It is the form which one may denote as
metaphorical thinking; the nature and meaning of
metaphor is what we must start with if we want to find,
on the one hand, the unity of the verbal and the mythical
worlds and, on the other, their difference.

It has frequently been noted that the intellectual link
between language and myth is metaphor; but in the
precise definition of the process, and even in regard to
the general direction it is supposed to take, theories are
widely at variance. The real source of metaphor is sought
now in the construction of language, now in mythic
imagination; sometimes it is supposed to be speech,
which by its originally metaphorical nature begets myth,
and is its eternal source; sometimes, on the contrary,
the metaphorical character of words is regarded as a
legacy which language has received from myth and holds
in fee. Herder, in his prize essay on the origin of speech,
emphasized the mythic aspect of all verbal and proposi-

tional conceptions. "As all nature sounds; so to Man, creature of sense, nothing could seem more natural than that it lives, and speaks, and acts. A certain savage sees a tree, with its majestic crown; the crown rustles! That is stirring godhead! The savage falls prostrate and worships! Behold the history of sensuous Man, that dark web, in its becoming, out of *verbis nomina*—and the easiest transition to abstract thought! For the savages of North America, for instance, everything is still animate; everything has its genius, its spirit. That it was likewise among Greeks and orientals, may be seen from their oldest dictionary and grammar—they are, as was all nature to their inventor, a pantheon! A realm of living, acting creatures. . . . The driving storm, the gentle zephyr, the clear fountain and the mighty ocean—their whole mythology lies in those treasure troves, in *verbis* and *nominibus* of the ancient languages; and the earliest dictionary was thus a sounding pantheon."[79]

The romantics followed the way indicated by Herder; Schelling, too, sees in language a "faded mythology," which preserves in formal and abstract distinctions what mythology still treats as living, concrete differences.[80] Exactly the opposite course was taken by the "comparative mythology" that was attempted in the second half of the nineteenth century, especially by Adalbert Kuhn and Max Müller. Since this school adopted the *methodological* principle of basing mythological comparisons on linguistic comparisons, the *factual* primacy of verbal concepts over mythic ones seemed to them to be implied in their procedure. Thus mythology appeared as a result of language. The "root metaphor" underlying all mythic

[79] "Ueber den Ursprung der Sprache," *Werke* (ed. Suphan), V, pp. 53 f.
[80] Schelling, "Einleitung in die Philosophie der Mythologie," *Sämtliche Werke*, 2nd div., I, p. 52.

formulations was regarded as an essentially verbal phenomenon, the basic character of which was to be investigated and understood. The homonymity or assonance of denotative terms was supposed to break and direct the way for mythic fantasy.

"Let us consider, then, that there was, necessarily and really, a period in the history of our race when all the thoughts that went beyond the narrow horizon of our everyday life had to be expressed by means of metaphors, and that these metaphors had not yet become what they are to us, mere conventional and traditional expressions, but were felt and understood half in their original and half in their modified character. . . . Whenever any word, that was at first used metaphorically, is used without a clear conception of the steps that led from its original to its metaphorical meaning, there is danger of mythology; whenever those steps are forgotten and artificial steps put in their places, we have mythology, or, if I may say so, we have diseased language, whether that language refers to religious or secular interests. . . . What is commonly called mythology is but a part of a much more general phase through which all language has at one time or other to pass."[81]

Before one can attempt any decision between these antagonistic theories, this battle for the priority of language over mythology or myth over language, the basic concept of metaphor requires scrutiny and definition. One can take it in a narrow sense, in which it comprises only the *conscious* denotation of one thought content by the name of another which resembles the former in some respect, or is somehow analogous to it. In that case, metaphor is a genuine "translation"; the two concepts

[81] Max Müller, *Lectures on the Science of Language*, second series (New York: Scribner, Armstrong & Co., 1875), pp. 372-376.

between which it obtains are fixed and independent meanings, and betwixt them, as the given *terminus a quo* and *terminus ad quem*, the conceptual process takes place, which causes the transition from one to the other, whereby one is semantically made to stand proxy for the other. Any attempt to probe the generic causes of this conceptual and nominal substitution, and to explain the extraordinarily wide and variegated use of this sort of metaphor (i.e., the conscious identification of avowedly diverse objects), especially in primitive forms of thinking and speaking, leads one back to an essential attitude of mythic thought and feeling. Heinz Werner, in his study of the origins of metaphor, has presented a very plausible argument for the supposition that this particular kind of metaphor, the circumlocution of one idea in terms of another, rests on quite definite motives arising from the magical view of the world, and more especially from certain name and word taboos.[82]

But such a use of metaphor clearly presupposes that both the ideas and their verbal correlates are already given as definite quantities; only if these elements, as such, are verbally fixed and defined can they be exchanged for one another. Such transposition and substitution, which operate with a previously known vocabulary as their material, must be clearly distinguished from that genuine "radical metaphor" which is a condition of the very formulation of mythic as well as verbal conceptions. Indeed, even the most primitive verbal utterance requires a transmutation of a certain cognitive or emotive experience into sound, i.e., into a medium that is foreign to the experience, and even quite disparate; just as the simplest mythical form can arise only

---

[82] Heinz Werner, *Die Ursprünge der Metapher* (Leipzig, 1919), esp. chap. 3, pp. 74 ff.

by virtue of a transformation which removes a certain impression from the realm of the ordinary, the everyday and profane, and lifts it to the level of the "holy," the sphere of mythico-religious "significance." This involves not merely a transference, but a real μετάβασις εἰς ἄλλο γένος; in fact, it is not only a transition to another category, but actually the creation of the category itself.

If, now, one were to ask which of these two types of metaphor begets the other—whether the metaphorical expressions in speech are produced by the mythic point of view, or whether, on the contrary, this point of view could arise and develop only on the basis of language— the foregoing considerations show that this question is really specious. For, in the first place, we are not dealing here with a temporal relation of "before" and "after," but with the logical relation between the forms of language and of myth, respectively; with the way the one conditions and determines the other. This determination, however, can be conceived only as reciprocal. Language and myth stand in an original and indissoluble correlation with one another, from which they both emerge but gradually as independent elements. They are two diverse shoots from the same parent stem, the same impulse of symbolic formulation, springing from the same basic mental activity, a concentration and heightening of simple sensory experience. In the vocables of speech and in primitive mythic figurations, the same inner process finds its consummation: they are both resolutions of an inner tension, the representation of subjective impulses and excitations in definite objective forms and figures. As Usener emphatically said: "It is not by any volition that the name of a thing is determined. People do not invent some arbitrary sound-complex, in order to introduce it as the sign of a certain object, as one might do with a token. The spiritual excitement caused by some object which presents itself in the outer world furnishes both the occasion and the means of its denomination. Sense impressions are what the self receives from its encounter with the not-self, and the liveliest of these naturally strive for vocal expression; they are the bases of the separate appellations which the speaking populace attempts."[83]

Now this genesis corresponds precisely, feature for feature, with that of the "momentary gods." Similarly, the significance of linguistic and mythic metaphors, respectively, will reveal itself, so that the spiritual power embodied in them may be properly understood, only as we trace them back to their common origin; if one seeks this significance and power in that peculiar concentration, that "intensification" of sense experience which underlies all linguistic as well as all mythico-religious formulations.

If we take our departure once more from the contrast which theoretical or "discursive" conception presents, we shall find indeed that the different *directions* which the growth of logical (discursive) and mythic-linguistic conception, respectively, have followed, may be seen just as clearly in their several *results*. The former begins with some individual, single perception, which we expand, and carry beyond its original bounds, by viewing it in more and more relationships. The intellectual process here involved is one of *synthetic supplementation*, the combination of the single instance with the totality, and its completion in the totality. But by this relationship with the whole, the separate fact does not lose its concrete identity and limitation. It fits into the sum total of phenomena, yet remains set off from them as something

[83] Usener, *Götternamen*, p. 3.

independent and singular. The ever-growing relationship which connects an individual perception with others does not cause it to become merged with the others. Each separate "specimen" of a species is "contained" in the species; the species itself is "subsumed" under a higher genus; but this means, also, that they remain distinct, they do not coincide. This fundamental relation is most readily and clearly expressed in the scheme which logicians are wont to use for the representation of the hierarchy of concepts, the order of inclusion and subsumption obtaining among genera and species. Here the logical determinations are represented as geometric determinations; every concept has a certain "area" that belongs to it and whereby it is distinguished from other conceptual spheres. No matter how much these areas may overlap, cover each other or interpenetrate—each one maintains its definitely bounded location in conceptual space. A concept maintains its sphere despite all its synthetic supplementation and extension; the new relations into which it may enter do not cause its boundaries to become effaced, but lead rather to their more distinct recognition.

If, now, we contrast this form of logical conception by species and genera with the primitive form of mythic and linguistic conception, we find immediately that the two represent entirely different *tendencies* of thought. Whereas in the former a concentric expansion over ever-widening spheres of perception and conception takes place, we find exactly the opposite movement of thought giving rise to mythic ideation. The mental view is not widened, but compressed; it is, so to speak, distilled into a single point. Only by this process of distillation is the particular essence found and extracted which is to bear the special accent of "significance." All light is concentrated in one focal point of "meaning," while everything that lies outside these focal points of verbal or mythic conception remains practically invisible. It remains "unremarked" because, and in so far as, it remains unsupplied with any linguistic or mythic "marker." In the realm of discursive conception there reigns a sort of diffuse light—and the further logical analysis proceeds, the further does this even clarity and luminosity extend. But in the ideational realm of myth and language there are always, besides those locations from which the strongest light proceeds, others that appear wrapped in profoundest darkness. While certain contents of perception become verbal-mythical centers of force, centers of significance, there are others which remain, one might say, beneath the threshold of meaning. This fact, namely, that primitive mythical and linguistic concepts constitute such *punctiform* units, accounts for the fact that they do not permit of any further *quantitative* distinctions. Logical contemplation always has to be carefully directed toward the *extension* of concepts; classical syllogistic logic is ultimately nothing but a system of rules for combining, subsuming and superimposing concepts. But the conceptions embodied in language and myth must be taken not in extension, but in intension; not quantitatively, but qualitatively. Quantity is reduced to a purely casual property, a relatively immaterial and unimportant aspect. Two logical concepts, subsumed under the next-higher category, as their *genus proximum*, retain their distinctive characters despite the relationship into which they have been brought. In mythico-linguistic thought, however, exactly the opposite tendency prevails. Here we find in operation a law which might actually be called the law of the leveling and extinction of specific differences. Every part of a whole is the whole

itself; every specimen is equivalent to the entire species.
The part does not merely represent the whole, or the
specimen its class; they are identical with the totality to
which they belong; not merely as mediating aids to
reflective thought, but as genuine presences which actually contain the power, significance and efficacy of the
whole. Here one is reminded forcefully of the principle
which might be called the basic principle of verbal as well
as mythic "metaphor"—the principle of *pars pro toto*.
It is a familiar fact that all mythic thinking is governed
and permeated by this principle. Whoever has brought
any part of a whole into his power has thereby acquired
power, in the magical sense, over the whole itself. What
significance the part in question may have in the structure and coherence of the whole, what function it fulfills,
is relatively unimportant—the mere fact that it is or has
been a part, that it has been connected with the whole,
no matter how casually, is enough to lend it the full
significance and power of that greater unity. For instance,
to hold magical dominion over another person's body
one need only attain possession of his pared nails or
cut-off hair, his spittle or his excrement; even his shadow,
his reflection or his footprints serve the same purpose.
The Pythagoreans still observed the injunction to smooth
the bed soon after arising so that the imprint of the
body, left upon the mattress, could not be used to the
owner's detriment.[84] Most of what is known as "magic
of analogy" springs from the same fundamental attitude;
and the very nature of this magic shows that the concept
in question is not one of mere analogy, but of a real
identification. If, for instance, a rain-making ceremony
consists of sprinkling water on the ground to attract the

[84] Jamblichos, *Protreptichos* p. 108, 3, quoted after Deubner, *Magie
und Religion* (Freiburg, 1922), p. 8.

rain, or rain-stopping magic is made by pouring water on red hot stones where it is consumed amid hissing noise,[85] both ceremonies owe their true magical sense to the fact that the rain is not just represented, but is felt to be really present in each drop of water. The rain as a mythic "power," the "daemon" of the rain is actually there, whole and undivided, in the sprinkled or evaporated water, and is thus amenable to magical control.

This mystic relationship which obtains between a whole and its parts holds also between genus and species, and between the species and its several instances. Here, too, each form is entirely merged with the other; the genus or species is not only represented by an individual member of it, but lives and acts in it. If, under the totemistic conception of the world, a group or clan is organized by totems, and if its individual members take their names from the totem animal or plant, this is never a mere arbitrary division by means of conventional verbal or mythical "insignia," but a matter of genuine community of essence.[86] In other respects, too, wherever a genus is involved at all, it always appears to be wholly present and wholly effective. The god or daemon of vegetation lives in each individual sheaf of the harvest. Therefore, an ancient but still popular rural custom demands that the last sheaf be left out in the field; in this remnant, the power of the fertility-god is concentrated, from which the harvest of the coming year is to grow.[87] In Mexico and among the Cora Indians the corn-god is supposed to be present, fully and unrestrictedly, in every

[85] See Parkinson, *Thirty Years in the South Seas*, p. 7; quoted by Werner, *Die Ursprünge der Metapher*, p. 56.

[86] Cf. my study, *Die Begriffsform im mythischen Denken* (Leipzig, 1922), pp. 16ff.

[87] Cf. Mannhardt, *Wald= und Feldkulte*, 2nd ed. (Berlin, 1904-1905), I, 212ff.

stalk and even every grain of corn. The Mexican corn-goddess Chicomecoatl in her maidenhood is the green stalk, in her old age the corn harvest; but she is also each separate kernel and each particular dish. Likewise, there are several deities among the Coras who represent certain kinds of flowers, but are addressed as individual flowers. The same is true of all the Coras' demoniac creatures: the cicada, the cricket, the grasshopper, the armadillo are simply treated as so many individual wholes.[88] If, therefore, ancient rhetoric names as one of the principal types of metaphor the substitution of a part for the whole, or vice versa, it is easy enough to see how *this* sort of metaphor arises directly out of the essential attitude of the mythic mind. But it is equally clear that for mythic thinking there is much more in metaphor than a bare "substitution," a mere rhetorical figure of speech; that what seems to our subsequent reflection as a sheer transcription is mythically conceived as a genuine and direct identification.[89]

[88] See Preuss, in *Globus*, Vol. 87, p. 381; cf. esp. *Die Nayarit-Expedition*, Vol. I, pp. 47 ff.

[89] This is the more obviously valid if we consider that for mythic and magical thought there is no such thing as a mere picture, since every image embodies the "nature" of its object, i.e., its "soul" or "daemon." Cf., for example, Budge, *Egyptian Magic*, p. 65: "It has been said above that the name or the emblem or the picture of a god or a demon could become an amulet with power to protect him that wore it and that such power lasted as long as the substance of which it was made lasted, if the name, or emblem, or picture was not erased from it. But the Egyptians went a step further than this and they believed that it was possible to transmit to the figure of any man, or woman, or animal or living creature the soul of the being which it represented, and its qualities and attributes. The statue of a god in a temple contained the spirit of the god which it represented, and from time immemorial the people of Egypt believed that every statue and figure possessed an indwelling spirit." The same belief is held to this day among all "primitive" peoples. Cf., for instance, Hetherwick, "Some animistic beliefs among the Yaos of British Central Africa" (see footnote above, p. 70): "The photographic camera was at first an object of dread, and when it was turned upon a group of natives

In the light of this basic principle of mythic metaphor we can grasp and understand, somewhat more clearly, what is commonly called the metaphorical function of language. Even Quintilian pointed out that this function does not constitute any *part* of speech, but that it governs and characterizes all human talk; *paene quidquid loquimur figura est.* But if this is indeed the case—if metaphor, taken in this general sense, is not just a certain development of speech, but must be regarded as one of its essential conditions—then any effort to understand its function leads us back, once more, to the fundamental form of verbal *conceiving.* Such conceiving stems ultimately from that same process of concentration, the compression of given sense experiences, which originally initiates every single verbal concept. If we assume that this sort of concentration occurs by virtue of several experiences, and along several lines, so that two different perceptual complexes might yield the same sort of "essence" as their inner significance, which *gives* them their meaning, then at this very point we should expect that first and firmest of all the connections which language can establish; for, as the nameless simply has no existence in language, but tends to be completely obscured, so whatever things bear the *same* appellation appear absolutely similar. The similarity of the aspect fixed by the word causes all other heterogeneity among the perceptions in question to become more and more obscured, and finally to vanish altogether. Here again, a part usurps the place of the whole—indeed, it becomes and is the whole. By virtue of the "equivalence" principle, entities

___

they scattered in all directions with shrieks of terror . . . In their minds the *lisoka* (soul) was allied to the *chiwilili* or picture and the removal of it to the photographic plate would mean the disease or death of the shadeless body" (pp. 89 f.).

which appear entirely diverse in direct sense perception
or from the standpoint of logical classification may be
treated as similars in language, so that every statement
made about one of them may be transferred and applied
to the other. Preuss, in a characterization of magic-
complex thinking, says: "If the Cora Indian classes butter-
flies, quite absurdly, as birds, this means that all the
properties which he notes in the object are quite differ-
ently classified and related for him than they are for us
from our analytical, scientific point of view."[90] But the
apparent absurdity of this and other such classifications
disappears as soon as we realize that the formation of
these primary concepts was guided by language. If we
suppose that the element emphasized in the name, and
therefore in the verbal concept of "bird," as an essential
characteristic was the element of "flight," then by virtue
of this element and by its mediation the butterfly does
belong to the class of birds. Our own languages are still
constantly producing such classifications, which contra-
dict our empirical and scientific concepts of species and
genera, as for instance the denotation "butterfly" (Dutch
botervlieg), in some Germanic tongues called a "butter-
bird." And at the same time one can see how such
lingual "metaphors" react in their turn on mythic metaphor and prove to be an ever-fertile source for the latter.
Every characteristic property which once gave a point
of departure to qualifying conceptions and qualifying
appellations may now serve to merge and identify the
objects denoted by these names. If the visible image of
lightning, as it is fixed by language, is concentrated upon
the impression of "serpentine," this causes the lightning
to *become a snake*; if the sun is called "the heavenly
flier," it appears henceforth as an arrow or a bird—the

[90] Preuss, *Die geistige Kultur der Naturvölker* (Leipzig, 1914), p. 10.

sun-god of the Egyptian pantheon, for instance, who is represented with a falcon's head. For in this realm of thought there are no abstract denotations; every word is immediately transformed into a concrete mythical figure, a god or a daemon. Any sense impression, no matter how vague, if it be fixed and held in language, may thus become a starting point for the conception and denotation of a god. Among the names of the Lithuanian gods which Usener has listed, the snow-god Blizgulis, the "Shimmerer," appears beside the god of cattle, the "Roarer" Baubis; also in relation to these we find the god of bees, Birbullis the "Hummer," and the god of earthquake, the "Thresher" Drebkulys.[91] Once a "Roarer God" in this sense was conceived, he could not but be recognized in the most diverse guises; he was naturally and directly *heard*, in the voice of the lion as in the roaring of the storm and the thunder of the ocean. Again and again, in this respect, myth receives new life and wealth from language, as language does from myth. And this constant interaction and interpenetration attests the unity of the mental principle from which both are sprung, and of which they are simply different expressions, different manifestations and grades.

Yet in the advance of human mentality even this conjunction, close and essential though it seems to be, begins to disintegrate and dissolve. For language does not belong exclusively to the realm of myth; it bears within itself, from its very beginning, another power, the power of logic. How this power gradually waxes great, and breaks its way by means of language, we cannot undertake to set forth here. But in the course of that evolution, words are reduced more and more to the status of mere conceptual signs. And this process of

[91] Usener, *Götternamen*, pp. 85 ff., 114.

separation and liberation is paralleled by another: art, like language, is originally bound up entirely with myth. Myth, language and art begin as a concrete, undivided unity, which is only gradually resolved into a triad of independent modes of spiritual creativity. Consequently, the same mythic animation and hypostatization which is bestowed upon the words of human speech is originally accorded to *images*, to every kind of artistic representation. Especially in the magical realm, word magic is everywhere accompanied by picture magic.[92] The image, too, achieves its purely representative, specifically "aesthetic" function only as the magic circle with which mythical consciousness surrounds it is broken, and it is recognized not as a mythico-magical form, but as a particular sort of *formulation*.

But although language and art both become emancipated, in this fashion, from their native soil of mythical thinking, the ideal, spiritual unity of the two is reasserted upon a higher level. If language is to grow into a vehicle of thought, an expression of concepts and judgments, this evolution can be achieved only at the price of forgoing the wealth and fullness of immediate experience. In the end, what is left of the concrete sense and feeling content it once possessed is little more than a bare skeleton. But there is one intellectual realm in which the word not only preserves its original creative power, but is ever renewing it; in which it undergoes a sort of constant palingenesis, at once a sensuous and a spiritual reincarnation. This regeneration is achieved as language becomes an avenue of artistic expression. Here it recovers the fullness of life; but it is no longer a life mythically bound and fettered, but an aesthetically liberated life.

[92] For further details see the second volume of my *Philosophie der symbolischen Formen*, esp. pp. 54ff.

Among all types and forms of poetry, the lyric is the one which most clearly mirrors this ideal development. For lyric poetry is not only rooted in mythic motives as its beginning, but keeps its connection with myth even in its highest and purest products. The greatest lyric poets, for instance Hölderlin or Keats, are men in whom the mythic power of insight breaks forth again in its full intensity and objectifying power. But this objectivity has discarded all material constraints. The spirit lives in the word of language and in the mythical image without falling under the control of either. What poetry expresses is neither the mythic word-picture of gods and daemons, nor the logical truth of abstract determinations and relations. The world of poetry stands apart from both, as a world of illusion and fantasy—but it is just in this mode of illusion that the realm of pure feeling can find utterance, and can therewith attain its full and concrete actualization. Word and mythic image, which once confronted the human mind as hard realistic powers, have now cast off all reality and effectuality; they have become a light, bright ether in which the spirit can move without let or hindrance. This liberation is achieved not because the mind throws aside the sensuous forms of word and image, but in that it uses them both as *organs* of its own, and thereby recognizes them for what they really are: forms of its own self-revelation.

INDEX

PRIMITIVE MAN AS PHILOSOPHER
by Paul Radin

This standard anthropological work considers aspects of primitive thought from such typical primitive peoples as the Winnebago, Oglala Sioux, Maori, Baganda, Batak, Buin of Melanesia, Polynesians of Tahiti and Hawaii, Zuni, Ewe and many others. It examines both the conditioning of thought which each society places upon the individual, and the freedom which the individual has either to deviate from group belief or to form group belief. Intensive discussion is given to such methodological problems as determining cultural standards.

It covers primitive thought on such topics as the relation of a man to his fellows, the purpose of life, marital relations, freedom of thought, death, resignation, and analyzes intensively folk wisdom from many primitive peoples. It also considers more abstract aspects of thought such as the nature of reality, the structure of the ego, human personality, the systematization of ideas, the concept of gods, belief, and similar matters.

It is not a simple compendium of traits, ripped out of context, but a brilliant interpretation of myth and symbolism in terms of the meaning assigned to them in each culture. It is factual in approach, and quotes original primitive documents extensively. It does not tear ideas from their matrix, nor does it seek far-fetched interpretations in terms of preconceived psychological theories.

Throughout most of this interesting book, primitive men are allowed to speak for themselves. Most of the supporting data were obtained at first hand, much of it by the author himself in his contacts with primitive peoples.

Bibliography. Index. xviii + 402pp. 5⅜ x 8.

T392 Paperbound **$1.95**

SUBSTANCE AND FUNCTION,
EINSTEIN'S THEORY OF RELATIVITY

by Ernst Cassirer

In this double-volume, the great modern philosopher Cassirer establishes a philosophy of the exact sciences that is at once historically sound, philosophically mature, and scientifically impeccable. It propounds a general philosophical system in which Einstein's theory is seen to be only the latest and most radical fulfillment of the motives which are inherent in mathematical and physical science as such. It covers such topics as the concept of number, space and geometry, non-Euclidean geometry, traditional logic and scientific method, mechanism and motion, Mayer's methodology, the concept of energy, Richter's difinite proportions, relational concepts and activity of the ego, the psychology of relation. Einstein's relativity from epistemological standpoint, relativity and reality, and so on.

Bibliography. Index. Authorized translated by W. C. and M. C. Swabey. xii + 465pp. 5⅜ x 8.

Paperbound **$2.00**

ESSAYS IN EXPERIMENTAL LOGIC

by John Dewey

This volume is an unabridged unaltered reprinting of the 1916 edition of this modern classic of philosophy. Written with all Dewey's conciseness and sense for practical application, it contains fourteen of his most influential papers on various aspects of knowledge, reality, and epistemology.

The foundation of these papers on experimental logic is the theory that knowledge about anything implies a judgment, which in turn implies an inquiry or investigation of a sort. The presence of this "inquiry stage" implies that between the external world and knowledge there is an intermediate and mediating stage, which is in turn conditioned by other factors. Expanding upon this basis, these papers consider the relationship of thought and its subject matter, the antecedents and stimuli of thought, data and meanings, the objects of thought, control of ideas by facts and similar topics.

Three papers describe various kinds of philosophical realism, in which the thought of Bertrand Russell's OUR KNOWLEDGE OF THE EXTERNAL WORLD AS A FIELD FOR SCIENTIFIC METHOD is closely examined, while two other papers discuss Pragmatism, differentiating Dewey's position from that of James and Peirce. These essays present what is probably Dewey's most easily followed account of his own thought. The section entitled "Stages of Logical Thought" analyzes the role of scientific method in philosophy, while the final essay presents a striking theory of a logic of values.
Index. viii + 444pp. 5⅜ x 8.

ARISTOTLE'S THEORY OF POETRY AND THE FINE ARTS

edited by S. H. Butcher

This book contains the celebrated Butcher translation of Aristotle's POETICS, faced, page by page, with the complete Greek text (as reconstructed by Mr. Butcher from Greek, Latin and Arabic manuscripts). The editor's 300-page exposition and interpretation follows.

In his classic commentary, Butcher discusses with insight, sympathy and great learning Aristotle's ideas and their importance in the history of thought and literature. His scholarly remarks cover art and nature, imitation as an aesthetic term, poetic truth, pleasure as the end of fine art, art and morality, the function of tragedy, the dramatic unities, the ideal tragic hero, plot and character, comedy, and poetic universality. A new 35-page introductory essay, "Aristotelian Literary Criticism" by John Gassner, discusses the validity of Aristotle's ideas today and their application to contemporary literature.

"No edition with commentary can be recommended to English readers with such confidence as Butcher's," George Saintsbury. "One of the finest treatises on aesthetic theory — neither the literature nor the criticism of the past 40 years has rendered Aristotelian criticism irrelevant or obsolete," MODERN SCHOOLMAN. "An intellectual adventure of the most stimulating kind," NEW YORK TIMES.

Fourth edition. Bibliography. New introduction by John Gassner. Indexes. lxxvi + 421pp. 5⅜ x 8.

T42 Paperbound $1.95

LANGUAGE, TRUTH AND LOGIC by A. J. Ayer

First published in 1936, this first full-length presentation in English of the Logical Positivism of Carnap, Neurath, and others has gone through 10 printings to become a classic of thought and communication. It not only surveys one of the most important areas of modern thought; it also shows you how to apply analytical methods to your own field of work and dispel the confusion that arises from imperfect understanding of the uses of language. A first-rate antidote for fuzzy thought and muddled writing, this remarkable book has helped philosophers, writers, speakers, teachers, students, and general readers alike.

Mr. Ayer sets up specific tests by which you can easily evaluate statements of ideas. You will also learn how to distinguish ideas that cannot be verified by experience — those expressing religious, moral, or aesthetic experience, those expounding theological or metaphysical doctrine, and those dealing with a *priori* truth. The basic thesis of this work is that philosophy should not squander its energies upon the unknowable, but should perform its proper function in criticism and analysis.

PARTIAL CONTENTS: Elimination of metaphysics, Function of philosophy. Nature of philosophic analysis. The a *priori* Truth and probability. Critique of ethics and theology. The self and the common world. Solutions of outstanding philosophical disputes.

"A delightful book...I should like to have written it myself," Bertrand Russell.

Index. 160 pp. 5⅜ x 8.   T10 Paperbound **$1.25**

Best introduction to classical philosophy

HISTORY OF ANCIENT PHILOSOPHY

by W. Windelband

Windelband's HISTORY OF ANCIENT PHILOSOPHY has served generations of scholars as the best introduction and survey volume to Greek and Roman philosophy. It combines rigorously exact scholarship, insight into the difficulties of the student, a genius for easily followed presentation with a remarkably complete coverage of persons, movements, and ideas.

After an introduction discussing ancient philosophy in general and the intellectual life of Greece in the 7th and 6th centuries B.C., the author discusses the Ionian speculators and Pythagoras. He then analyzes the Milesians (Thales, Anaximander, Anaximenes), Heraclitus, the Eleatics, Empedocles, Anaxagoras, Leucippus, the Pythagoreans, the Sophists, Socrates, and other early schools and personalities. 20 pages are then devoted to an analysis of Democritus, 50 pages to Plato, and 70 pages to Aristotle.

The remainder of the book discusses later classical philosophy. The Peripatetics, Stoics, Epicureans are covered in detail, as are the Skeptics and the Middle Platonists. Neoplatonism is described in terms of Plotinus, Jamblichus and Proclus, while a special chapter gives a brief discussion of those Christian Apologists who used philosophic techniques, the more important Gnostics, and Origen.

Background information is supplied for each philosopher and his thought, while an evaluated bibliography of thousands of entries is given in separate sections within the text. It covers all the basic work in the historiography of philosophy up to 1900.

Translated by H. E. Cushman, from 2nd German edition. xv + 393pp. 5⅜ x 8.   Paperbound **$1.75**

ORIENTAL RELIGIONS IN ROMAN PAGANISM
by Franz Cumont

This study by the great Belgian historian Franz Cumont describes one aspect of the cultural meeting of east and west in the Early Roman Empire. It describes the great pagan religions of the orient, and tells how their religious thought and ceremonial permeated, altered, and revivified Roman paganism.

It provides a coverage of all the more important eastern religions of the time, from their first appearance in Rome, 204 B.C., when the great Mother of the Gods was first imported from Syria:

> The ecstatic cults of Phrygia and Syria; the worship of Cybele, the Magna Mater, Attis, Adonis; their orgies and mutilatory rites.
> The mysteries of Egypt; the worship of Serapis, Isis, Osiris, their closely hidden secret rites, redemption ceremonies.
> The dualism of Persia; the elevation of cosmic evil to a full and equal partnership with the deity; the mysteries of Mithra.
> The worship of Hermes Trismegistos, and the documents ascribed to him; Sabazios, Ishtar, Astarte.
> The magic, thaumaturgy, judicial astrology of the ancient near east.
> The emotional and intellectual impact of the great civilized traditions of Egypt and Babylonia upon still barbarian Europe.

Cumont's ORIENTAL RELIGIONS IN ROMAN PAGANISM is the best general picture, on an intermediate level, of this important moment in cultural history. It is also of great value in analyzing an era which shared certain cultural problems with our own time.

Introduction by Grant Showerman. 55pp. of notes, with extensive evaluated bibliography. Translated from 2nd French edition. Index. xxiv + 298pp. 5⅜ x 8.   Paperbound **$1.75**

MIND AND THE WORLD-ORDER
by C. I. Lewis

This well-known work by Professor Lewis of Harvard University outlines a theory of knowledge in terms of a new system, "conceptual pragmatism." Building upon the work of Peirce, James, and Dewey it takes into account both recent philosophic thought and the implications of modern mathematics.

Starting with the assumption that there are two systems of truth (abstract mathematical certainty, and secondly, empirical truth—or application of abstract truth to sense experiences) the author demonstrates that the traditional understanding of the a priori must be abandoned.

Chapters are included about philosophy, metaphysics, philosophic method; the given element in experience; pure concepts; common concepts; knowledge of objects; relativity of knowledge; the a priori, traditional conceptions; the nature of the a priori; the a priori and the empirical; the empirical and the problem; experience and order. Appendixes cover natural science and abstract concepts, applicability of abstract conceptual systems to experience, and similar topics.

This book is of interest not only to the specialist in philosophy, but also to the reader interested in the common ground where mathematics and philosophy meet.

xiv + 446pp. 5⅜ x 8.   Paperbound **$1.95**

SCIENCE THEORY AND MAN, Erwin Schrödinger. Complete unabridged reissue of SCIENCE AND THE HUMAN TEMPERAMENT plus an additional essay: "What Is an Elementary Particle?" Nobel Laureate Schrödinger discusses such topics as nature of scientific method, the nature of science, chance and determinism, science and society, conceptual models for physical entities, elementary particles and wave mechanics. Presentation is popular. "Fine practical preparation for a time when laws of nature, human institutions . . . are undergoing a critical examination without parallel," Waldemar Kaempffert, N. Y. TIMES. 192pp. 5⅜ x 8.   T428 Paperbound **$1.35**

BRIDGES AND THEIR BUILDERS, D. B. Steinman & S. R. Watson. Engineers, historians, and every person who has ever been fascinated by great spans will find this book an endless source of information and interest. Greek and Roman structures, Medieval bridges, modern classics such as the Brooklyn Bridge, and the latest developments in the science are retold by one of the world's leading authorities on bridge design and construction. BRIDGES AND THEIR BUILDERS is the only comprehensive and accurate semi-popular history of these important measures of progress in print. New, greatly revised, enlarged edition. 23 photos; 26 line-drawings. Index. xvii + 401pp. 5⅜ x 8.   T431 Paperbound **$1.95**

BIOLOGY, NATURAL HISTORY & TRAVEL

TREES OF THE EASTERN AND CENTRAL UNITED STATES AND CANADA, W. M. Harlow. A revised edition of a standard middle-level guide to native trees and important escapes. More than 140 trees are described in detail, and illustrated with more than 600 drawings and photographs. Supplementary keys will enable the careful reader to identify almost any tree he might encounter. xiii + 288pp. 5⅜ x 8.
T395 Paperbound **$1.35**

INTRODUCTION TO THE STUDY OF EXPERIMENTAL MEDICINE, Claude Bernard. The only major work of Claude Bernard now available in English, this classical records Bernard's efforts to transform physiology into an exact science. He examines the roles of chance and error and incorrect hypothesis in leading to scientific truth and describes many classic experiments on the action of curare, carbon monoxide, and other poisons, the functions of the pancreas, the glycogenic function of the liver, and many others. Introduction. Foreword by I. B. Cohen. xxv + 266pp. 5⅜ x 8.   T400 Paperbound **$1.50**

THE ORIGIN OF LIFE, A. I. Oparin. The first modern statement of the theory that life evolved from complex nitro-carbon compounds. A historical introduction covers theories of the origin of life from the Greeks to modern times and then the techniques of biochemistry as applied to the problem by Dr. Oparin. The exposition presupposes a knowledge of chemistry but can be read with profit by everyone interested in this absorbing question. Bibliography. Index. xxv + 270pp. 5⅜ x 8.
S213 Paperbound **$1.75**

A SHORT HISTORY OF ANATOMY AND PHYSIOLOGY FROM THE GREEKS TO HARVEY, C. Singer. An intermediate history formerly entitled THE EVOLUTION OF ANATOMY, this work conveys the thrill of discovery as the nature of the human body is gradually clarified by hundreds of scientists from the Greeks to the Renaissance. Diogenes, Hippocrates, and other early workers, up to Leonardo da Vinci, Vesalius, Harvey, and others, with 139 illustrations from medieval manuscripts, classical sculpture, etc. Index. 221pp. 5⅜ x 8.   T389 Paperbound **$1.75**

THE BEHAVIOUR AND SOCIAL LIFE OF HONEYBEES, Ronald Ribbands. The most comprehensive, lucid, and authoritative book on bees. How bees communicate, how they tell fellow workers exactly how far away stores of food are, how individual bees learn their duties in the hive, and all the complex patterns and motivations. Much of the material is the result of very recent research by Mr. Ribbands and others. "A 'MUST' for every scientist, experimenter, and educator, and a happy and valuable selection for all interested in the honeybee," AMERICAN BEE JOURNAL. 690 item bibliography. Indices. 127 illustrations; 11 photographic plates. 352pp.   S410 Clothbound **$4.50**

TRAVELS OF WILLIAM BARTRAM, edited by Mark Van Doren. One of the 18th century's most delightful books; an excellent source of first-hand material on American geography, anthropology, and natural history. Many descriptions of early Indian tribes are our only source of information. "The mind of a scientist with the soul of a poet," John Livingston Lowes. 13 original illustrations and maps. Edited with an introduction by Mark Van Doren. 448pp. 5⅜ x 8.   T13 Paperbound **$2.00**

SAILING ALONE AROUND THE WORLD, Captain Joshua Slocum. A great modern classic in a convenient inexpensive edition. Captain Slocum's account of his single-handed voyage around the world in a 34 foot boat which he rebuilt himself. A nearly unparalled feat of seamanship told with vigor, wit, imagination, and great descriptive power. "A nautical equivalent of Thoreau's account," Van Wyck Brooks. 67 illustrations. 308pp. 5⅜ x 8.   T326 Paperbound **$1.00**

EARTH SCIENCES

THE BIRTH AND DEVELOPMENT OF THE GEOLOGICAL SCIENCES, F. D. Adams. The most complete and thorough history of the earth sciences in print. Geological thought from earliest recorded times to the end of the 19th century — covers over 300 early thinkers and systems: fossils and hypothetical explanations of them, vulcanists vs. neptunists, figured stones and paleontology, generation of stones, and similar topics. 91 illustrations, including medieval, renaissance woodcuts, etc. 632 footnotes and bibliographic notes. Index. 511pp. 5⅜ x 8.   T5 Paperbound **$2.00**

URANIUM PROSPECTING, H. L. Barnes. A clear, practical book about uranium prospecting by a professional geologists with first-hand field experience. Hundreds of important facts about minerals, geological occurrence, tests, detectors, sampling, assays, claiming and developing, government regulations. Index. Glossary of technical terms. Annotated bibliography. x + 117pp. 5⅜ x 8.
T309 Paperbound **$1.00**

DE RE METALLICA, Georgius Agricola. Written over 400 years ago, for 200 years the most authoritative work on production of metals; still one of the most beautiful and fascinating volumes in the history of science. 12 books, exhaustively annotated, give a wonderfully lucid and vivid picture of the history of mining, selection of sites, types of deposits, excavating pits, sinking shafts, ventilating, pumps, crushing machinery, assaying, smelting, refining metals, making salt, alum, nitre, glass, and many other topics. This definitive edition contains all 289 of the 16th century woodcuts which made the original an artistic masterpiece. A superb gift for geologists, engineers, libraries, artists, and historians. Biographical, historical introductions. Translated by Herbert & L. H. Hoover. Bibliography, survey of ancient authors. Indices. 289 illustrations. 672pp. 6¾ x 10¾. Deluxe library edition.
S6 Clothbound **$10.00**

MUSIC

A GENERAL HISTORY OF MUSIC, Charles Burney. A detailed coverage of music from the Greeks up to 1789, with full information on all types of music: sacred and secular, vocal and instrumental, operatic and symphonic. Theory, notation, forms, instruments, innovators, composers, performers, typical and important works, and much more in an easy, entertaining style. Burney travelled over much of Europe and spoke with hundreds of authorities and composers so that this work is more than a compilation of records . . . it is a living work of careful and first-hand scholarship. A recent NEW YORK TIMES review said, "Surprisingly few of Burney's statements have been invalidated by modern research . . . still of great value." Edited and corrected by Frank Mercer. 35 figures. Indices. 1915pp. 5½ x 8½.
2 volumes. T36 The set, Clothbound **$12.50**

JOHANN SEBASTIAN BACH, Philipp Spitta. The complete and unabridged text of the definitive study of Bach. Written some 70 years ago, it is still unsurpassed for its coverage of nearly all aspects of Bach's life and work. There could hardly be a finer non-technical introduction to Bach's music than the detailed, lucid analyses which Spitta provides for hundreds of individual pieces. 26 solid pages are devoted to the B minor mass, for example, and 30 pages to the glorious St. Matthew Passion. This monumental set also includes a major analysis of the music of the 18th century: Buxtehude, Pachelbel, etc. "Unchallenged as the last word on one of the supreme geniuses of music," Hohn Barkham, SATURDAY REVIEW SYNDICATE. Total of 1819pp. 2 volumes. Heavy cloth binding. 5⅜ x 8.
The set, T252 Clothbound **$10.00**

A DICTIONARY OF HYMNOLOGY, John Julian. This exhaustive and scholarly work has become known as an invaluable source of hundreds of thousands of important and often difficult to obtain facts on the history and use of hymns in the western world. More than 30,000 entries on individual hymns, giving authorship, date and circumstances of composition, publication, textual variations, location of texts, translations, denominational and ritual usage, etc. Biographies of more than 9,000 hymn writers, and essays on important topics such as Christmas carols and children's hymns, and much other unusual and valuable information. A 200 page double-columned index of first lines — the largest in print. Total of 1786 pages in two reinforced clothbound volumes. 6¼ x 9¼. The set, T333 Clothbound **$15.00**

STRUCTURAL HEARING: TONAL COHERENCE IN MUSIC, Felix Salzer. Written by a pupil of the late Heinrich Schenker, this is not only the most thorough exposition in English of the Schenker method but also extends the Schenker approach to include modern music, music of the middle ages, and renaissance music. It explores the phenomenon of tonal organization by means of a detailed analysis and discussion of more than 500 musical pieces. It casts new light for the reader acquainted with harmony upon the understanding of musical compositions, problems of musical coherence, and connection between theory and composition. "Has been the foundation on which all teaching in music theory has been based at this college," Leopold Mannes, President of The Mannes College of Music. 2 volumes. Total of 658pp. 6½ x 9¼.
The set, S418 Clothbound **$8.00**

PUZZLES, ENTERTAINMENT, ETC.

MATHEMATICS, MAGIC AND MYSTERY, Martin Gardner. Why do card tricks work? How do magicians perform astonishing mathematical feats? How is stage mind-reading possible? This is the first book length study explaining the application of probability, set theory, theory of numbers, topology, etc., to many startling tricks. Non-technical, accurate, detailed. 115 sections discuss tricks with cards, dice, coins, knots, geometrical vanishing illusions, how a Curry square "demonstrates" that the sum of the parts may be greater than the whole, and dozens of others. 135 illustrations. xii + 174pp. 5⅜ x 8.
T335 Paperbound **$1.00**

MATHEMATICAL PUZZLES FOR BEGINNERS AND ENTHUSIASTS, G. Mott-Smith. 188 mathematical puzzles based on algebra, dissection of plane figures, permutations and probability, that will test and improve your powers of inference and interpretation. The Odic Force, The Spider's Cousin, Ellipse Drawing, theory and strategy of card and board games. 100 pages of detailed mathematical explanations. Appendix of primes, square roots, etc. 135 illustrations. 2nd revised edition. 248pp. 5⅜ x 8.
T198 Paperbound **$1.00**

LEARN CHESS FROM THE MASTERS, F. Reinfeld. Formerly titled CHESS BY YOURSELF, this book contains 10 games which you play against such masters as Marshall, Bronstein, Najdorf, and others, and an easy system for grading each move you make against a variety of other possible moves. Detailed annotations reveal the principles of the game through actual play. 91 diagrams. viii + 144pp. 5⅜ x 8.
T362 Paperbound **$1.00**

REINFELD ON THE END GAME IN CHESS, F. Reinfeld. Formerly titled PRACTICAL END-GAME PLAY, this book contains clear, simple analyses of 62 end games by such masters as Alekhine, Tarrasch, Marshall, Morphy, Capablanca, and many others. Primary emphasis is on the general principles of transition from, middle play to end play. This book is unusual in analyzing weak or incorrect moves to show how error occurs and how to avoid it. Covers king and pawn, minor piece, queen endings, weak squares, centralization, tempo moves, and many other vital factors. 62 diagrams. vi + 177pp. 5⅜ x 8.
T417 Paperbound **$1.25**

101 PUZZLES IN THOUGHT AND LOGIC, C. R. Wylie, Jr. Brand new problems you need no special knowledge to solve! Take the kinks out of your mental "muscles" and enjoy solving murder problems, the detection of lying fishermen, the logical identification of color by a blindman, and dozens more. Introduction with simplified explanation of general scientific method and puzzle solving. 128pp. 5⅜ x 8.
T367 Paperbound **$1.00**

THE COMPLETE NONSENSE OF EDWARD LEAR. This is the only complete edition of this master of gentle madness available at a popular price. A BOOK OF NONSENSE, NONSENSE SONGS, MORE NONSENSE SONGS AND STORIES in their entirety with all the old favorites that have delighted children and adults for years. The Dong With A Luminous Nose, The Jumblies, The Owl and the Pussycat, and hundreds of other bits of wonderful nonsense. 214 limericks, 3 sets of Nonsense Botany, 5 Nonsense Alphabets, 546 drawings by Lear himself, and much more. 320pp. 5⅜ x 8.
T167 Paperbound **$1.00**

28 SCIENCE FICTION STORIES OF H. G. WELLS. Two full unabridged novels, MEN LIKE GODS and STAR BEGOTTEN, plus 26 short stories by the master science-fiction writer of all time! Stories of space, time, invention, exploration, future adventure. PARTIAL CONTENTS: Men like Gods, The Country of the Blind, In the Abyss, The Crystal Egg, The Man Who Could Work Miracles, A Story of the Days to Come, The Valley of Spiders, and 21 more! 5⅜ x 8.
T265 Clothbound **$3.95**

SEVEN SCIENCE FICTION NOVELS, H. G. Wells. Full unabridged texts of 7 science-fiction novels of the master. Ranging from biology, physics, chemistry, astronomy, to sociology and other studies, Mr. Wells extrapolates whole worlds of strange and intriguing character. "One will have to go far to match this for entertainment, excitement, and sheer pleasure," NEW YORK TIMES. Contents: THE TIME MACHINE, THE ISLAND OF DR. MOREAU, THE FIRST MEN IN THE MOON, THE INVISIBLE MAN, THE WAR OF THE WORLDS, THE FOOD OF THE GODS, IN THE DAYS OF THE COMET. 1015pp. 5⅜ x 8.
T264 Clothbound **$3.95**

FIVE ADVENTURE NOVELS OF H. RIDER HAGGARD. All the mystery and adventure of darkest Africa captured accurately by a man who lived among Zulus for years, and who knew African ethnology and folkways as did few of his contemporaries. They have been regarded as examples of the very best high adventure by such critics as George Orwell, Andrew Lang and Kipling. Contents: SHE, KING SOLOMON'S MINES, ALLAN QUATERMAIN, ALLAN'S WIFE, MAIWA'S REVENGE. 821pp. 5⅜ x 8.
T108 Clothbound **$3.95**

MATHEMAGIC, MAGIC PUZZLES, AND GAMES WITH NUMBERS, R. V. Heath. More than 60 new puzzles and stunts based on the properties of numbers. Easy techniques for multiplying large numbers mentally, revealing hidden numbers magically, finding the date of any day in any year, and dozens more. Edited by J. S. Meyer. 76 illustrations. 128pp. 5⅜ x 8.
T110 Paperbound **$1.00**

WIN AT CHECKERS, M. Hopper. (Formerly CHECKERS). The former World's Unrestricted Checker Champion discusses the principles of the game, expert's shots and traps, problems for the beginner, standard openings, locating your best move, the end game, opening "blitzkrieg" moves, ways to draw when you are behind your opponent, etc. More than 100 detailed questions and answers anticipate your problems. Appendix. 75 problems with solutions and diagrams. Index. 79 figures. xi + 107pp. 5⅜ x 8.
T363 Paperbound **$1.00**

HOUDINI ON MAGIC, Harry Houdini. One of the greatest magicians of modern times explains his most prized secrets. How locks are picked, with illustrated picks and skeleton keys; how a girl is sawed into twins; how to walk through a brick wall — Houdini's explanations of 44 stage tricks with many diagrams. Also included is a fascinating discussion of great magicians of the past and the story of his fight against fraudulent mediums and spiritualists. Edited by W. B. Gibson and M. N. Young. Bibliography. 155 figures, photos. xv + 280pp. 5⅜ x 8.
T384 Paperbound **$1.00**

THE BOOK OF MODERN PUZZLES, G. L. Kaufman. A completely new series of puzzles as fascinating as crossword and deduction puzzles but based upon different principles and techniques. Simple 2-minute teasers, word labyrinths, design and pattern puzzles, logic and observation puzzles — over 150 brainrackers. Answers to all problems. 116 illustrations. 192pp. 5⅜ x 8. T143 Paperbound **$1.00**

NEW WORD PUZZLES, G. L. Kaufman. 100 ENTIRELY NEW puzzles based on words and their combinations. Chess words, based on the moves of the chess king; design-onyms; symmetrical designs made of synonyms; rhymed double-crostics; syllable sentences; addle letter anagrams; alphagrams; linkograms; and many others all brand new. Full solutions. Space to work problems. 196 figures. vi + 122pp. 5⅜ x 8.
T344 Paperbound **$1.00**

MATHEMATICAL RECREATIONS, M. Kraitchik. One of the most thorough compilations of unusual mathematical problems for beginners and advanced mathematicians. Historical problems from Greek, Medieval, Arabic, Hindu sources. 50 pages devoted to pastimes derived from figurate numbers, Mersenne numbers, Fermat numbers, primes and probability. 40 pages of magic, Euler, Latin, panmagic squares. 25 new positional and permutational games of permanent value: fairy chess, latruncles, reversi, jinx, ruma, lasca, tricolor, tetrachrome, etc. Complete rigorous solutions. Revised second edition. 181 illustrations. 330pp. 5⅜ x 8.
T163 Paperbound **$1.75**

MATHEMATICAL EXCURSIONS, H. A. Merrill. Even if you hardly remember your high school math, you'll enjoy the 90 stimulating problems. Little effort. Many useful shortcuts and diversions not generally known are included: division by inspection, Russian peasant multiplication, memory systems for pi, building odd and even magic squares, square roots by geometry, dyadic systems, and many more. Solutions to difficult problems. 50 illustrations. 145pp. 5⅜ x 8.   T350 Paperbound **$1.00**

PUZZLE QUIZ AND STUNT FUN, J. Meyer. The solution to party doldrums. 238 challenging puzzles, stunts and tricks. Mathematical puzzles like The Clever Carpenter, Atom Bomb; mysteries and deductions like The Bridge of Sighs, The Nine Pearls, Dog Logic; observation puzzles like Cigarette Smokers, Telephone Dial; over 200 others including magic squares, tongue twisters, puns, anagrams, and many others. All problems solved fully. 250pp. 5⅜ x 8.   T337 Paperbound **$1.00**

MAGIC TRICKS & CARD TRICKS, W. Jonson. Two books bound as one. 52 tricks with cards, 37 tricks with coins, bills, eggs, smoke, ribbons, slates, etc. Details on presentation, misdirection, and routining will help you master such famous tricks as the Changing Card, Card in the Pocket, Four Aces, Coin Through the Hand, Bill in the Egg, Afghan Bands, and over 75 others. If you follow the lucid exposition and key diagrams carefully, you will finish these two books with an astonishing mastery of magic. 106 figures. 224pp. 5⅜ x 8.   T909 Paperbound **$1.00**

CRYPTANALYSIS, H. F. Gaines. Formerly entitled ELEMENTARY CRYPTANALYSIS. The best book in print on cryptograms and their solution. Covers all major techniques of the past, and contains much that is not generally known except to experts. Full details about concealment, substitution, and transposition ciphers; periodic mixed alphabets, multafid, Kasiski and Vignere methods, Ohaver patterns, Playfair, and scores of other topics. 6 language letter and word frequency appendix. 167 problems, now furnished with solutions. Index. 173 figures. vi + 230pp. 5⅜ x 8.
                                                                  T97 Paperbound **$1.95**

FLATLAND, E. A. Abbott. A science-fiction classic of life in a 2-dimensional world that is also a first-rate introduction to such aspects of modern science as relativity and hyperspace. Political, moral, satirical, and humorous overtones have made FLATLAND fascinating reading for thousands. 7th edition. 16 illustrations. 128pp. 5⅜ x 8.   T1 Paperbound **$1.00**

PARTY GAMES, M. Moyes. Over 80 old favorites and new entertainments in this sparkling collection for adults and children. All are easy, safe, fun, and require no special equipment. Organizing the party, warming-up games, performing, games, dance games, children's games, forfeits, and others. Large and small groups, family and guest, everybody loves games! 26 illustrations. 80pp. 5 x 7¼.
                                                                  T941 Paperbound **75¢**

WIN AT CHESS, F. Reinfeld. 300 practical chess situations from actual tournament play to sharpen your chess eye and test your skill. Traps, sacrifices, mates, winning combinations, subtle exchanges, show you how to WIN AT CHESS. Short notes and tables of solutions and alternative moves help you evaluate your progress. Learn to think ahead playing the 'crucial moments' of historic games. 300 diagrams. Notes and solutions. Formerly titled CHESS QUIZ. vi + 120pp. 5⅜ x 8.
                                                                  T438 Paperbound **$1.00**

HOW TO FORCE CHECKMATE, F. Reinfeld. Formerly titled CHALLENGE TO CHESSPLAYERS, this is an invaluable collection of 300 lightning strokes selected from actual masters' play, which will demonstrate how to smash your opponent's game with strong decisive moves. No board needed — clear, practical diagrams and easy-to-understand solutions. Learn to plan up to three moves ahead and play a superior end game. 300 diagrams. 111pp. 5⅜ x 8.   T439 Paperbound **$1.25**

MORPHY'S GAMES OF CHESS, edited by Philip W. Sergeant. You can put boldness into your game by following the brilliant, forceful moves of the man who has been called the greatest chess player of all time. 300 of Morphy's best games, carefully annotated, reveal Morphy's principles. Unabridged reissue of the latest revised edition. Bibliography. New introduction by Fred Reinfeld. Annotations and introduction by Sergeant. Index. 235 diagrams. x + 352pp. 5⅜ x 8.
                                                                  T386 Paperbound **$1.75**

THE ART OF THE STORY-TELLER, M. L. Shedlock. Regarded by librarians, story-tellers, and educators as the finest, most lucid book on the subject. The nature of the story, difficulties of communicating stories to children, artifices used in story-telling, how to obtain and maintain the effect of the story, and the elements to seek or avoid in selecting material. A 99 page selection of most effective stories. Extensive bibliography of further material. xxi + 320pp. 5⅜ x 8.   T245 Paperbound **$3.50**

CRYPTOGRAPHY, L. D. Smith. An excellent introductory work on ciphers and their solution, the history of secret writing, and actual methods and problems in such techniques as transposition and substitution. Appendices describe the enciphering of Japanese, the Baconian biliteral cipher, and contain frequency tables and a bibliography for further study. Over 150 problems with solutions. 160pp. 5⅜ x 8.   T247 Paperbound **$1.00**

LANGUAGE

NEW RUSSIAN-ENGLISH AND ENGLISH-RUSSIAN DICTIONARY, M. A. O'Brien. Over 70,000 entries in new orthography! Idiomatic uses, colloquialisms. Irregular verbs, perfective and imperfective aspects, regular and irregular sound changes, and other features. One of the few dictionaries where accent changes within the conjugation of verbs and the declension of nouns are fully indicated. "One of the best," Prof. E. J. Simmons, Cornell. First names, geographical terms, bibliography, etc. 738pp. 4½ x 6¼.   T208 Paperbound **$2.00**

MONEY CONVERTER AND TIPPING GUIDE FOR EUROPEAN TRAVEL, C. Vomacka. Currency regulations and tipping for every European country including Iron Curtain countries, Israel, Egypt, and Turkey. Complete conversion tables for every country from U.S. to foreign and vice versa. Only source of such information as phone rates, postal rates, clothing sizes, duty-free imports, and dozens of other valuable topics. 128pp. 3½ x 5¼. **T260 Paperbound 65¢**

MONEY CONVERTER AND TIPPING GUIDE FOR TRAVEL IN THE AMERICAS (including the United States and Canada), C. Vomacka. The information you need for informed and confident travel in North and South America. U. S. to foreign and foreign to U. S. currency conversion tables for every country. Special section covers over 250 tipping situations in the U.S. Tipping, postal and telephone rates, customs regulations, and much more is covered for all countries. 128pp. 3½ x 5¼. **T261 Paperbound 65¢**

DUTCH-ENGLISH AND ENGLISH-DUTCH DICTIONARY, F. G. Renier. For travel, literary, scientific or business Dutch; the most convenient, practical and comprehensive dictionary on the market. More than 60,000 entries, shades of meaning, colloquialisms, idioms, compounds and technical terms. Dutch and English ·strong and irregular verbs. This is the only dictionary in its size and price range that indicates the gender of nouns. New orthography for use with older books. xviii + 571pp. 5½ x 6¼. **T224 Clothbound $2.50**

LEARN DUTCH!, F. G. Renier. The most satisfactory and most easily used grammar of modern Dutch. The student is gradually led from simple lessons in pronunciation, through translation, finally to a mastery of spoken and written Dutch. Grammatical principles are clearly explained while a useful, practical vocabulary is introduced in easy exercises and readings. It is used and recommended by the Fulbright Committee in the Netherlands. Phonetic appendices. Over 1200 exercises; Dutch-English, English-Dutch vocabularies. 181pp. 4¼ x 7¼. **T441 Clothbound $1.75**

LISTEN & LEARN

FRENCH SPANISH GERMAN ITALIAN

LISTEN & LEARN is the only language record course designed especially to meet your travel and everyday needs. It is available in separate sets for FRENCH, SPANISH, GERMAN, or ITALIAN, and each set contains 3 ten-inch 33-1/3 rpm long-playing records — 1½ hours of recorded speech by eminent native speakers who are professors at Columbia, New York University, Queens College. Check the following special features found only in LISTEN & LEARN:

- **Dual-language recording. 812 selected phrases and sentences,** over 3200 words, spoken first in English, then in their foreign language equivalents. A suitable pause follows each foreign phrase, allowing you time to repeat the expression. You learn by unconscious assimilation.

- **128-page manual** contains everything on the records, plus a simple phonetic pronunciation guide.

- **Indexed for convenience. The only set on the market** that is completely indexed. No more puzzling over where to find the phrase you need. Just look in the rear of the manual.

- **Practical.** No time wasted on material you can find in any grammar. LISTEN & LEARN covers central core material with phrase approach. Ideal for the person with limited learning time.

- **Living, modern expressions,** not found in other courses. Hygienic products, modern equipment, shopping — expressions used every day, like "nylon" and "air-conditioned."

- **Limited objective.** Everything you learn, no matter where you stop, is immediately useful. You have to finish other courses, wade through grammar and vocabulary drill, before they help you.

- **High-fidelity recording.** LISTEN & LEARN records equal in clarity and surface-silence any record on the market costing up to $6 per record.

41 different categories covering all your travel wants — Greetings, introductions, social conversations . . . Making yourself understood . . . Useful words, phrases, sentences . . . Passing customs, checking baggage . . . Buying travel tickets . . . Flying, train travel, boats, buses, streetcars, taxis, subways . . . Automobile travel, repairs, parts . . . At a nightclub, restaurant . . . Menus: breakfast, soups, entrees, vegetables, salads, fruits, drinks, desserts . . . Sports, sightseeing, concerts, dancing . . . Cashing checks . . . Cameras, photography, films . . . Drugstores, doctors, dentists, medicines . . . Barber shops, beauty parlors, laundries, dry cleaning . . . Telephoning, postal services . . . Time, numbers, dates, months, seasons . . . and many more, including the largest collection of street and shop signs in print anywhere.

"Excellent . . . the spoken records . . . impress me as being among the very best on the market," **Prof. Mario Pei,** Dept. of Romance Languages, Columbia University. "Inexpensive and well-done . . . it would make an ideal present," CHICAGO SUNDAY TRIBUNE. "More genuinely helpful than anything of its kind which I have previously encountered," **Sidney Clark,** well-known author of "ALL THE BEST" travel books.

UNCONDITIONAL GUARANTEE. Try LISTEN & LEARN, then return it within 10 days for full refund if you are not satisfied. The only course on the market guaranteed after you actually use it.

LISTEN & LEARN comes in 4 useful modern languages — FRENCH, SPANISH, GERMAN, or ITALIAN — one language to each set of 3 ten-inch records, (33-1/3 rpm). 128 page manual. Album.

Spanish	the set **$4.95**	German	the set **$4.95**
French	the set **$4.95**	Italian	the set **$4.95**

SAY IT language phrase books

These handy phrase books (128 to 196 pages each) make grammatical drills unnecessary for an elementary knowledge of a spoken foreign language. Covering most matters of travel and everyday life each volume contains:

Over 1000 phrases and sentences in immediately useful forms — foreign language plus English.
Modern usage designed for Americans. Specific phrases like, "Give me small change," and "Please call a taxi."
Simplified phonetic transcription you will be able to read at sight.
The only completely indexed phrase books on the market.
Covers scores of important situations: — Greetings, restaurants, sightseeing, useful expressions, etc.

These books are prepared by native linguists who are professors at Columbia, N.Y.U., Fordham and other great universities. Use them independently or with any other book or record course. They provide a supplementary living element that most other courses lack. Individual volumes in:

French 60¢	**German 60¢**	**Italian 60¢**
Russian 60¢	**Portuguese 75¢**	**Spanish 60¢**
Hebrew 60¢	**Norwegian 75¢**	**Swedish 60¢**
Japanese 60¢	**Polish 75¢**	**Modern Greek 60¢**
Dutch 75¢	**Esperanto 75¢**	**Yiddish 75¢**
English for Spanish-speaking people 60¢		
English for Italian-speaking people 60¢		
English for German-speaking people 60¢		
Turkish 75¢		

Large clear type. 128-196 pages each. 3½ x 5¼.
Sturdy paper binding.

LITERATURE

WORLD DRAMA, B. H. Clark. 46 plays from Ancient Greece, Rome, Medieval Europe, France, Germany, Italy, England, Russia, Scandinavia, India, China. Japan, etc. — including classic authors like Aeschylus, Sophocles, Euripides, Aristophanes, Plautus, Marlowe, Jonson, Farquhar, Goldsmith, Cervantes, Moliere, Dumas, Goethe, Schiller, Ibsen, and many others. This creative collection avoids hackneyed material. Over 1/3 of this material is unavailable in any other current edition! "The most comprehensive collection of important plays from all literature available in English," SAT. REV. OF LITERATURE. Introduction. Reading lists. 2 volumes. 1364pp. 5⅜ x 8.
Vol. 1, T57 Paperbound **$2.00**
Vol. 2, T59 Paperbound **$2.00**

MASTERS OF THE DRAMA, John Gassner. The most comprehensive history of the drama in print, covering drama in every important tradition from the Greeks to the Near East, China, Japan, Medieval Europe, England, Russia, Italy, Spain, Germany, and dozens of other drama producing nations. This unsurpassed reading and reference work encompasses more than 800 dramatists and over 2000 plays, with biographical material, plot summaries, theatre history, etc. "Best of its kind in English," NEW REPUBLIC. Exhaustive 35 page bibliography. 77 photographs and drawings. Deluxe edition with reinforced cloth binding, headbands, stained top. xxii + 890pp. 5⅜ x 8.
T100 Clothbound **$5.95**

THE DRAMA OF LUIGI PIRANDELLO, D. Vittorini. All 38 of Pirandello's plays written between 1918 and 1935 are summarized and analyzed in this authorized study. Their cultural background, place in European dramaturgy, symbolic techniques, and plot structure are carefully examined. Foreword by Pirandello. Biography. Bibliography. xiii + 350pp. 5⅜ x 8.
T435 Paperbound **$1.98**

ARISTOTLE'S THEORY OF POETRY AND THE FINE ARTS, edited by S. H. Butcher. The celebrated Butcher translation of this great classic faced, page by page, with the complete Greek text. A 300 page introduction discussing Aristotle's ideas and their influence in the history of thought and literature, and covering art and nature, imitation as an aesthetic form, poetic truth, art and morality, tragedy, comedy, and similar topics. Modern Aristotelian criticism discussed by John Gassner. lxxvi + 421pp. 5⅜ x 8.
T41 Clothbound **$3.95**
T42 Paperbound **$2.00**

EUGENE O'NEILL: THE MAN AND HIS PLAYS, B. H. Clark. No source-book has previously been published on O'Neill's life and work. Clark analyzes each play from the early THE WEB to the recently produced MOON FOR THE MISBEGOTTEN and THE ICEMAN COMETH, revealing the environmental and dramatic influences necessary for a complete understanding of these important works. Bibliography. Appendices. Index. ix + 182pp. 5⅜ x 8.
T379 Paperbound **$1.25**

EPIC AND ROMANCE, W. P. Ker. Written by one of the foremost authorities on medieval literature, this is the standard survey of medieval epic and romance. It covers Teutonic epics, Icelandic sagas, Beowulf, French chansons de geste, the Roman de Troi, and many other important works of literature. It is an excellent account of a body of literature whose beauty and value has only recently come to be recognized. Index. xxiv + 398pp. 5⅜ x 8.
T355 Paperbound **$1.95**

FOUNDERS OF THE MIDDLE AGES, E. K. Rand. The best non-technical discussion of the transformation of Latin pagan culture into medieval civilization. Tertullian, Gregory, Jerome, Boethius, Augustine, the Neoplatonists, and many other literary men, educators, classicists, and humanists. A storehouse of information presented clearly and simply for the intelligent non-specialist. "Thoughtful, beautifully written," AMERICAN HISTORICAL REVIEW. "Extraordinarily accurate," Richard McKeon, THE NATION. ix + 365pp. 5⅜ x 8.
T369 Paperbound **$1.85**

ORIENTALIA

CHRISTIAN AND ORIENTAL PHILOSOPHY OF ART, A. K. Coomaraswamy. A unique fusion of philosopher, orientalist, art historian, and linguist discusses the true function of aesthetics in art, symbolism, intellectual and philosophic backgrounds, the role of traditional culture in enriching art, the nature of medieval art, the nature of folklore, the beauty of mathematics, and similar topics. 2 illustrations. Bibliography. 148pp. 5⅜ x 8. T378 Paperbound **$1.25**

TRANSFORMATION OF NATURE IN ART, A. K. Coomaraswamy. Unabridged reissue of a basic work upon Asiatic religious art and philosophy of religion. The theory of religious art in Asia and Medieval Europe (exemplified by Meister Eckhart) is analyzed and developed. Indian Medieval aesthetic manuals, symbolic language in philosophy, the origin and use of images in India, and many other fascinating and little known topics. Glossaries of Sanskrit and Chinese terms. Bibliography. 41pp of notes. 245pp. 5⅜ x 8. T368 Paperbound **$1.75**

ORIENTAL RELIGIONS IN ROMAN PAGANISM, F. Cumont. A study of the cultural meeting of east and west in the Early Roman Empire. Important eastern religions from their first appearance in Rome, 204 B.C., when the Great Mother of the Gods was first brought over from Syria. The ecstatic cults of Syria and Phrygia — Cybele, Attis, Adonis, their orgies and mutilatory rites; the mysteries of Egypt — Serapis, Isis, Osiris; the dualism of Persia, the elevation of cosmic evil to equal stature with the deity, Mithra; worship of Hermes Trismegistus; Ishtar, Astarte; the magic of the ancient Near East, etc. Introduction. 55pp. of notes; extensive bibliography. Index. xxiv + 298pp. 5⅜ x 8. T321 Paperbound **$1.75**

THE MYSTERIES OF MITHRA, F. Cumont. The definitive coverage of a great ideological struggle between the west and the orient in the first centuries of the Christian era. The origin of Mithraism, a Persian mystery religion, and its associaion with the Roman army is discussed in detail. Then utilizing fragmentary monuments and texts, in one of the greatest feats of scholarly detection, Dr. Cumont reconstructs the mystery teachings and secret doctrines, the hidden organization and cult of Mithra. Mithraic art is discussed, analyzed, and depicted in 70 illustrations. 239pp. 5⅜ x 8. T323 Paperbound **$1.85**

YOGA, H. P. Shastri. A disciple of the Indian saint Shri Dada, and founder of an important center of classical Yoga, the author gives a lucid, comprehensive account of yoga as practised according to Shankara's Ideal Monism. This is neither an occult book nor a shallow popularization; it is a careful introduction to one of the most important Indian philosophical methods of achieving self-discipline and self-understanding through mental and physical exercise. Glossary. Passages from yoga literature. 6 figures. 96pp. 5 x 7¼. T975 Paperbound **75¢**

ANTHROPOLOGY, SOCIAL SCIENCES, ETC.

THE IDEA OF PROGRESS, J. B. Bury. Practically unknown before the Reformation, the idea of progress has since become one of the central concepts of western civilization. Prof. Bury analyzes its evolution in the thought of Greece, Rome, the Middle Ages, the Renaissance, to its flowering in all branches of science, religion, philosophy, industry, art, and literature, during and following the 16th century. Introduction by Charles Beard. Index. xl + 357pp. 5⅜ x 8. T39 Clothbound **$3.95**
T40 Paperbound **$1.95**

PRIMITIVE MAN AS PHILOSOPHER, P. Radin. A standard anthropological work covering primitive thought on such topics as the purpose of life, marital relations, freedom of thought, symbolism, death, resignation, the nature of reality, personality, gods, and many others. Drawn from factual material gathered from the Winnebago, Oglala Sioux, Maori, Baganda, Batak, Zuni, among others, it interprets strictly within the original framework. Extensive selections of original primitive documents. Bibliography. Index. xviii + 402pp. 5⅜ x 8. T392 Paperbound **$2.00**

PRIMITIVE RELIGION, P. Radin. A thorough treatment of the supernatural and the influences that have shaped religious expression in primitive societies. Ranging over Arunta, Ashanti, Aztec, Bushman, Crow, Fijian, etc., Africa, Australia, Pacific Islands, the Arctic, North and South America, Prof. Radin integrates modern psychology, comparative religion, and economic thought with first-hand accounts gathered by himself and other scholars of primitive initiations, training of the shaman, and other fascinating topics. "Excellent," NATURE (London). New author's preface. Bibliographic notes. Index. x + 322pp. 5⅜ x 8. T393 Paperbound **$1.85**

THE GIFT OF LANGUAGE, M. Schlauch. Formerly titled THE GIFT OF TONGUES, this is a middle-level survey that avoids both superficiality and pedantry. It covers such topics as linguistic families, word histories, grammatical processes in such foreign languages as Aztec, Ewe, and Bantu, semantics, language taboos, and dozens of other fascinating and important topics. Especially interesting is an analysis of the word-coinings of Joyce, Cummings, Stein and others in terms of linguistics. 232 bibliographic notes. Index. viii + 342pp. 5⅜ x 8. T243 Paperbound **$1.85**

PHILOSOPHY

GUIDE TO PHILOSOPHY, C. E. M. Joad. Does free will exist? Is there plan in the universe? How do we know and validate our knowledge? Such opposed solutions as subjective idealism and realism, chance and teleology, vitalism and logical positivism, are evaluated and the contributions of the great philosophers from the Greeks to moderns like Russell, Whitehead, and others, are considered in the context of each problem. "The finest introduction," BOSTON TRANSCRIPT. Index. Classified bibliography. 592pp. 5⅜ x 8.   T297 Paperbound **$2.00**

THE PHILOSOPHY OF HEGEL, W. T. Stace. The first detailed analysis of Hegel's thought in English, this is especially valuable since so many of Hegel's works are out of print. Dr. Stace examines Hegel's debt to Greek idealists and the 18th century and then proceeds to a careful description and analysis of Hegel's first principles, categories, reason, dialectic method, his logic, philosophy of nature and spirit, etc. Index. Special 14 x 20 chart of Hegelian system. x + 526pp. 5⅜ x 8.
T253 Clothbound **$3.95**
T254 Paperbound **$2.00**

ARISTOTLE, A. E. Taylor. A brilliant, searching non-technical account of Aristotle and his thought written by a foremost Platonist. It covers the life and works of Aristotle; classification of the sciences; logic, first philosophy, matter and form; causes; motion and eternity; God; physics; metaphysics; and similar topics. Bibliography. New index compiled for this edition. 128pp. 5⅜ x 8.
T279 Clothbound **$2.75**
T280 Paperbound **$1.00**

HISTORY OF ANCIENT PHILOSOPHY, W. Windelband. Perhaps the clearest survey of Greek and Roman philosophy. Discusses ancient philosophy in general, intellectual life in Greece in the 7th and 6th centuries B.C., Thales, Anaximander, Anaximenes, Heraclitus, the Eleatics, Empedocles, Anaxagoras, Leucippus, the Pythagoreans, the Sophists, Socrates, Democritus (20 pages), Plato (50 pages), Aristotle (70 pages), the Peripatetics, Stoics, Epicureans, Sceptics, Neo-platonists, Christian Apologists, etc. 2nd German edition translated by H. E. Cushman. xv + 393pp. 5⅜ x 8.   T357 Paperbound **$1.75**

LANGUAGE AND MYTH, E. Cassirer. Analyzing the non-rational elements in culture, Cassirer demonstrates that beneath both language and myth lies an unconscious "grammar" of experience whose categories and canons are not those of logical thought. His analyses of seemingly diverse phenomena such as Indian metaphysics, the Melanesian "mana," the Naturphilosophie of Schelling, modern poetry, etc., are profound without being pedantic. Introduction and translation by Susanne Langer. Index. x + 103pp. 5⅜ x 8.   T51 Paperbound **$1.25**

SUBSTANCE AND FUNCTION, EINSTEIN'S THEORY OF RELATIVITY, E. Cassirer. In this double-volume, Cassirer develops a philosophy of the exact sciences that is historically sound, philosophically mature, and scientifically impeccable. Such topics as the concept of number, space and geometry, non-Euclidean geometry, traditional logic and scientific method, mechanism and motion, energy, relational concepts, degrees of objectivity, the ego, Einstein's relativity, and many others are treated in detail. Authorized translation by W.C. and M. C. Swabey. xii + 465pp. 5⅜ x 8.   T50 Paperbound **$2.00**

THE PHILOSOPHICAL WORKS OF DESCARTES. Definitive English edition of all major philosophical works and letters of René Descartes. All of his revolutionary insights, from his famous "Cogito ergo sum" to his detailed account of contemporary science and his astonishingly fruitful concept that all phenomena of the universe (except mind) could be reduced to clear laws by the use of mathematics. An excellent source for the thought of men like Hobbes, Arnauld, Gassendi, etc. Translated by E. S. Haldane and G. Ross. Introductory notes. Index. Total of 842pp. 5⅜ x 8.
T71 Vol. 1, Paperbound **$2.00**
T72 Vol. 2, Paperbound **$2.00**

ESSAYS IN EXPERIMENTAL LOGIC, J. Dewey. Based upon the theory that knowledge implies a judgement, which in turn implies an inquiry, these papers consider the inquiry stage in terms of: the relationship of thought and subject matter, antecedents of thought, data and meanings. 3 papers examine Bertrand Russell's thought, while 2 others discuss pragmatism and a final essay presents a new theory of the logic of values. Index. viii + 444pp. 5⅜ x 8.   T73 Paperbound **$1.95**

THE PHILOSOPHY OF HISTORY, G. W. F. Hegel. One of the great classics of western thought which reveals Hegel's basic principle: that history is not chance but a rational process, the realization of the Spirit of Freedom. Ranges from the oriental cultures of subjective thought to the classical subjective cultures, to the modern absolute synthesis where spiritual and secular may be reconciled. Translation and introduction by J. Sibree. Introduction by C. Hegel. Special introduction for this edition by Prof. Carl Friedrich. xxxix + 447pp. 5⅜ x 8.   T112 Paperbound **$1.85**

THE WILL TO BELIEVE and HUMAN IMMORTALITY, W. James. Two complete books bound as one. THE WILL TO BELIEVE discusses the interrelations of belief, will, and intellect in man; chance vs. determinism, free will vs. fate, pluralism vs. monism; the philosophies of Hegel and Spencer, and more. HUMAN IMMORTALITY examines the question of survival after death and develops an unusual and powerful argument for immortality. Two prefaces. Index. Total of 429pp. 5⅜ x 8.
T294 Clothbound **$3.75**
T291 Paperbound **$1.75**

INTRODUCTION TO SYMBOLIC LOGIC, S. Langer. No special knowledge of math required. You start with simple symbols and advance to a knowledge of the Boole-Schroeder and Russell-Whitehead systems. Forms, logical structure, classes, the calculus of propositions, logic of the syllogism, etc., are all covered. "One of the clearest and simplest introductions," MATHEMATICS GAZETTE. Second enlarged, revised edition. 368pp. 5⅜ x 8. S164 Paperbound **$1.75**

MIND AND THE WORLD-ORDER, C. I. Lewis. Building upon the work of Peirce, James, and Dewey, Professor Lewis outlines a theory of knowledge in terms of "conceptual pragmatism." Dividing truth into abstract mathematical certainty and empirical truth, the author demonstrates that the traditional understanding of the a priori must be abandoned. Detailed analyses of philosophy, metaphysics, method, the "given" in experience, knowledge of objects, nature of the a priori, experience and order, and many others. Appendices. xiv + 446pp. 5⅜ x 8. T359 Paperbound **$1.95**

THE GUIDE FOR THE PERPLEXED, Maimonides. One of the great philosophical works of all time and a necessity for everyone interested in the philosophy of the Middle Ages in the Jewish, Christian, and Moslem traditions. Maimonides develops a common meeting-point for the Old Testament and the Aristotelian thought which pervaded the medieval world. 2nd revised edition. Complete unabridged Friedländer translation. 55 page introduction to Maimonides' life, period, etc., with an important summary of the GUIDE. Index. lix + 414pp. 5⅜ x 8. T351 Paperbound **$1.85**

THE PHILOSOPHICAL WRITINGS OF PEIRCE, edited by J. Buchler. Formerly THE PHILOSOPHY OF PEIRCE), a carefully integrated exposition of Peirce's complete system composed of selections from his own work. Symbolic logic, scientific method, theory of signs, pragmatism, epistemology, chance, cosmology, ethics, and many other topics are treated by one of the greatest philosophers of modern times. xvi + 386pp. 5⅜ x 8. T216 Clothbound **$5.00**
T217 Paperbound **$1.95**

SCEPTICISM AND ANIMAL FAITH, G. Santayana. To eliminate difficulties in the traditional theory of knowledge, Santayana distinguishes between the independent existence of objects and the essence our mind attributes to them. Scepticism is thereby established as a form of belief, and animal faith is shown to be a necessary condition of knowledge. Belief, classical idealism, intuition, memory, symbols, literary psychology, and much more, discussed with unusual clarity and depth. Index. xii + 314pp. 5⅜ x 8. T235 Clothbound **$3.50**
T236 Paperbound **$1.50**

THE ANALYSIS OF MATTER, B. Russell. Logical analysis of physics, prerelativity physics, causality, scientific inference, Weyl's theory, tensors, invariants and physical interpretations, periodicity, and much more is treated with Russell's usual brilliance. "Masterly piece of clear thinking and clear writing," NATION AND ATHENAEUM. "Most thorough treatment of the subject," THE NATION. Introduction. Index. 8 figures. viii + 408pp. 5⅜ x 8. T231 Paperbound **$1.95**

THE SENSE OF BEAUTY, G. Santayana. A revelation of the beauty of language as well as an important philosophic treatise, this work studies the "why, when, and how beauty appears, what conditions an object must fulfill to be beautiful, what elements of our nature make us sensible of beauty, and what the relation is between the constitution of the object and the excitement of our susceptibility." "It is doubtful if a better treatment of the subject has since been published," PEABODY JOURNAL. Index. ix + 275pp. 5⅜ x 8. T237 Clothbound **$2.85**
T238 Paperbound **$1.00**

THE CHIEF WORKS OF SPINOZA. Spinoza's most important philosophical works. Vol. I: The Theologico-Political Treatise and the Political Treatise. Vol. II: On The Improvement Of Understanding, The Ethics, Selected Letters. Profound and enduring ideas on God, the universe, pantheism, society, religion, the state, democracy, the mind, emotions, freedom, and the nature of man, which influenced Goethe, Hegel, Schelling, Coleridge, Whitehead, and many others. Introduction. 2 volumes. 862pp. 5⅜ x 8. T249 Vol. I, Paperbound **$1.50**
T250 Vol. II, Paperbound **$1.50**

TRAGIC SENSE OF LIFE, M. de Unamuno. The acknowledged masterpiece of one of Spain's most influential thinkers. Between the despair at the inevitable death of man and all his works and the desire for something better, Unamuno finds that "saving incertitude" that alone can console us. This dynamic appraisal of man's faith in God and in himself has been called, "A masterpiece," by the ENCYCLOPAEDIA BRITANNICA. xxx + 332pp. 5⅜ x 8. T257 Paperbound **$1.95**

PHILOSOPHY AND CIVILIZATION IN THE MIDDLE AGES, M. de Wulf. This semi-popular survey covers aspects of medieval intellectual life such as religion, philosophy, science, the arts, etc. It also covers feudalism vs. Catholicism, rise of the universities, mendicant orders, monastic centers, and similar topics. Unabridged. Bibliography. Index. viii + 320pp. 5⅜ x 8. T284 Paperbound **$1.75**

AN INTRODUCTION TO SCHOLASTIC PHILOSOPHY, Prof. M. de Wulf. Formerly entitled SCHOLASTICISM OLD AND NEW, this examines the central scholastic tradition from St. Anslem, Albertus Magnus, Thomas Aquinas, up to Suarez in the 17th century. The relation of scholasticism to ancient and medieval philosophy and science is clear and easily followed. The second part of the book considers the modern revival of scholasticism, the Louvain position, relations with Kantianism and Positivism. Unabridged. xvi + 271pp. 5⅜ x 8. T296 Clothbound **$3.50**
T283 Paperbound **$1.75**

HISTORY OF MEDIAEVAL PHILOSOPHY, M. de Wulf. An unabridged reproduction of this standard history of medieval philosophy from the 4th to 12th centuries A.D. Covers St. Augustine, Boethius, John Scotus Erigena, St. Anselm, the school of Chartres, Abelard, Hugh of St. Victor, John of Salisbury, Peter Lombard, and scores of others including dualists, canonists, jurists, mystics like Dionysius Areopagitica, St. Bernard, Joachim of Flores, and others. Byzantine, Arabic and Jewish philosophy, and the scholastic tradition covered in detail. Classified bibliography of thousands of items. "The best treatment of the subject in English," Richard McKeon. Recommended by SHAW'S LIST OF BOOKS FOR COLLEGE LIBRARIES; STANDARD CATALOG FOR PUBLIC LIBRARIES. Indexed. xviii + 317pp. Volume 1 only.
T285 Clothbound **$4.00**

A HISTORY OF MODERN PHILOSOPHY, H. Höffding. An exceptionally clear and detailed coverage of western philosophy from the Renaissance to the end of the 19th century. Major and minor men such as Pomponazzi, Bodin, Boehme, Telesius, Bruno, Copernicus, da Vinci, Kepler, Galileo, Bacon, Descartes, Hobbes, Spinoza, Leibniz, Wolff, Locke, Newton, Berkeley, Hume, Erasmus, Montesquieu, Voltaire, Diderot, Rousseau, Lessing, Kant, Herder, Fichte, Schelling, Hegel, Schopenhauer, Comte, Mill, Darwin, Spencer, Hartmann, Lange and many others are discussed in terms of theory of knowledge, logic, cosmology, and psychology. Index. 2 volumes, total of 1159pp. 5⅜ x 8.
T117 Vol. 1, Paperbound **$2.00**
T118 Vol. 2, Paperbound **$2.00**

LANGUAGE, TRUTH AND LOGIC, A. J. Ayer. A clear, careful analysis of the basic ideas of Logical Positivism. Building on the work of Schlick, Russell, Carnap, and the Viennese School, Mr. Ayer develops a detailed exposition of the nature of philosophy, science, and metaphysics; the Self and the World; logic and common sense, and other philosophic concepts. An aid to clarity of thought as well as the first full-length development of Logical Positivism in English. Introduction by Bertrand Russell. Index. 160pp. 5⅜ x 8.
T10 Paperbound **$1.25**

PSYCHOLOGY

SEX IN PSYCHO-ANALYSIS (formerly CONTRIBUTIONS TO PSYCHO-ANALYSIS), S. Ferenczi. Written by an associate of Freud, this volume presents countless insights on such topics as impotence, transference, analysis and children, dreams, symbols, obscene words, masturbation and male homosexuality, paranoia and psycho-analysis, the sense of reality, hypnotism and therapy, and many others. Also includes full text of THE DEVELOPMENT OF PYSCHO-ANALYSIS by Ferenczi and Otto Rank. Two books bound as one. Total of 406pp. 5⅜ x 8.
T324 Paperbound **$1.85**

THE PRINCIPLES OF PSYCHOLOGY, William James. The full long course, unabridged, of one of the great classics of Western literature and science. Wonderfully lucid descriptions of mental activity, the stream of thought, consciousness, time perception, memory, imagination, emotions, reason, abnormal phenomena, and similiar topics. Original contributions are integrated with the work of such men as Berkeley, Binet, Mills, Darwin, Hume, Kant, Royce, Schopenhauer, Spinoza, Locke, Descartes, Galton, Wundt, Lotse, Herbart, Fechner and scores of others. All contrasting interpretations of mental phenomena are examined in detail — introspective analysis, philosophical interpretation, and experimental research. "A classic," JOURNAL OF CONSULTING PSYCHOLOGY. "The main lines are as valid as ever," PSYCHOANALYTICAL QUARTERLY. "Standard reading . . . a classic of interpretation," PSYCHIATRIC QUARTERLY. 94 illustrations. 1408pp. 2 volumes. 5⅜ x 8.
Vol. 1, T381 Paperbound **$2.00**
Vol. 2, T382 Paperbound **$2.00**

ARTS AND CRAFTS

STICKS AND STONES, Louis Mumford. A survey of forces that have conditioned American architecture and altered its forms. The medieval tradition in early New England villages; the Renaissance influence and rise of the merchant class; the classical influence of Jefferson's time; the "Mechanicsvilles" of Poe's generation; the Brown Decades; the philosophy of the Imperial facade; and finally the modern machine age. "A truly remarkable book," SAT. REV. OF LITERATURE. 2nd revised edition. 21 illustrations. xvii + 228pp. 5⅜ xx 8.
T202 Paperbound **$1.60**

THE AUTOBIOGRAPHY OF AN IDEA, Louis Sullivan. The pioneer architect whom Frank Lloyd Wright called "the master" records the crystallization of his opinions and theories, the growth of his organic theory of architecture that still influences American designers and architects. This volume contains 34 full-page plates of his finest architecture. Unabridged reissue of 1924 edition. New introduction by R. M. Line. Index. xiv + 335pp. 5⅜ x 8.
T281 Paperbound **$1.85**

THE MATERIALS AND TECHNIQUES OF MEDIEVAL PAINTING, D. V. Thompson. Based on years of study of medieval manuscripts and laboratory analysis of medieval paintings, this book discusses carriers and grounds, binding media, pigments, metals used in painting, etc. Considers relative merits of painting al fresco and al secco, the processing of coloring materials, burnishing, and many other matters. Preface by Bernard Berenson. Index. 239pp. 5⅜ x 8.
T327 Paperbound **$1.85**

WILD FOWL DECOYS, J. Barber. The standard work on this fascinating branch of folk art, this book describes duck decoys of all sorts ranging from Indian mud and grass devices to the realistic carved wooden decoys invented in Revolutionary days and still in use. Collectors information about styles, types, and periods as well as detailed information on producing your own decoys is given in a lucid and entertaining style. Seven decoy paintings and sets of plans (14 new plates) have been added, making a total of 140 unusual and valuable illustrations (4 in color) for handycrafters, artists, hunters, and students of folk art. 281pp. 7⅞ x 10¾. Deluxe edition.
T11 Clothbound **$8.50**

METALWORK AND ENAMELLING, H. Maryon. Probably the best book ever written on the subject. Prepared by Herbert Maryon, F.S.A., of the British Museum, it tells everything necessary for home manufacture of jewelry, rings, ear pendants, bowls, and dozens of other objects. Clearly written chapters provide precise information on such topics as materials, tools, soldering, filigree, setting stones, raising patterns, spinning metal, repoussé work, hinges and joints, metal inlaying, damascening, overlaying, niello, Japanese alloys, enamelling, cloisonné, painted enamels, casting, polishing coloring, assaying, and dozens of other techniques. This is the next best thing to apprenticeship to a master metalworker. 363 photographs and figures. 374pp. 5½ x 8½. T183 Clothbound **$7.50**

PRINCIPLES OF ART HISTORY, H. Wölfflin. Analyzing such terms as ''baroque,'' ''classic,'' ''neoclassic,'' ''primitive,'' ''picturesque,'' and 164 different works by artists like Botticelli, van Cleve, Dürer, Hobbema, Holbein, Hals, Rembrandt, Titian, Brueghel, Vermeer, and many others, the author shows what really occurred between the 14th century primitives and the sophistication of the 18th century in terms of basic attitudes and philosophies. ''A remarkable lesson in the art of seeing,'' SAT. REV. OF LITERATURE. Translated from the 7th German edition. 150 illustrations. 254pp. 6⅛ x 9¼. T276 Paperbound **$2.00**

SHAKER FURNITURE, E. D. and F. Andrews. Far and away the most illuminating study of Shaker furniture and the principles of Shaker craftsmanship ever written. The results of 15 years of research in Shaker communities, archives, and collections, Chronology, craftsmanship, furniture, houses, shops, etc., of Shaker culture. Over 200 chairs, tables, desks, clocks, beds, benches, are illustrated by clear photographs. For everyone interested in Americana, antiques, art, American culture of fine arts. ''Mr. & Mrs. Andrews knows all there is to know about Shaker furniture,'' MARK VAN DOREN, NATION. 48 full page plates. 192pp. Deluxe cloth binding. 7⅞ x 10¾. T7 Clothbound **$6.00**

HANDBOOK OF ORNAMENT, F. S. Meyer. One of the largest collections of copyright-free traditional art. Over 3300 line cuts of Greek, Roman, Medieval, Islamic, Renaissance, Baroque, 18th and 19th century objects. 180 plates illustrate networks, Gothic tracery, geometric elements, flower and animal motifs, etc., while 100 plates illustrate decorative objects: chairs, thrones, cabinets, crowns, weapons, utensils, vases, jewelry, armor, heraldry, bottles, altars, and scores of other objects. Full text. 3300 illustrations. xiv + 548pp. 5⅜ x 8. T302 Paperbound **$2.00**

THREE CLASSICS OF ITALIAN CALLIGRAPHY, edited by Oscar Ogg. Complete reproductions of three famous calligraphic works by the greatest writing masters of the Renaissance: Arrighi's OPERINA and IL MODO, Tagliente's LO PRESENTE LIBRO, and Palatino's LIBRO NUOVO. These books present more than 200 complete alphabets and thousands of lettered specimens. The basic hand is Papal Chancery, but scores of other alphabets are also given: European and Asiatic local alphabets, foliated and ''art'' alphabets, scrolls, cartouches, borders, etc. Text is in Italian. Introduction. 245 plates. x + 272pp. 6⅛ x 9¼. T212 Paperbound **$1.95**

THE HISTORY AND TECHNIQUES OF LETTERING, A. Nesbitt. The only thorough inexpensive history of letter froms from the point of view of the artist. Mr. Nesbitt covers every major development in lettering from the ancient Egyptians to the present and illustrates each development with a complete alphabet. Such masters as Baskerville, Bell, Bodoni, Caslon, Koch, Kilian, Morris, Garamont, Jenson, and dozens of others are analyzed in terms of artistry and historical development. The author also presents a 65 page practical course in lettering, besides the full historical text. 89 complete alphabets; 165 additional lettered specimens. xvii + 300pp. 5⅜ x 8. T427 Paperbound **$2.00**

LETTERING AND ALPHABETS, J. A. Cavanagh. This unabridged reissue of LETTERING offers a full discussion, analysis, illustration of 89 basic hand lettering styles — styles derived from Caslons, Bodonis, Garamonds, Gothic, Black Letter, Oriental and many others. Upper and lower cases, numerals and common signs pictured. Hundreds of technical hints on make-up, construction, artistic validity, strokes, pens, brushes, white areas, etc. May be reproduced without permission! 89 complete alphabets; 72 lettered specimens. 121pp. 9¾ x 8. T53 Paperbound **$1.25**

THE HUMAN FIGURE IN MOTION, Eadweard Muybridge. The largest selection in print of Muybridge's famous high-speed action photos of the human figure in motion. 4789 photographs illustrate 162 different actions: men, women, children — mostly undraped — are shown walking, running, carrying various objects, sitting, lying down, climbing, throwing, arising, and performing over 150 other actions. Some actions are shown in as many as 120 photographs each. More than 500 action strips at shutter speeds as high as 1/6000th of a second! These are not posed shots, but true stopped motion. They show bone and muscles in situations that the human eye is not fast enough to capture. Earlier, smaller editions of these prints have brought $40 and more on the out-of-print market. ''A must for artists,'' ART IN FOCUS. ''An unparalled dictionary of action for all artists,'' AMERICAN ARTIST. 390 full-page plates, with 4789 photographs. Printed on heavy glossy stock. Reinforced binding with headbands. 7⅞ x 10⅝. T204 Clothbound **$10.00**

ANIMALS IN MOTION, Eadweard Muybridge. This is the largest collection of animal action photos in print. 34 different animals (horses, mules, oxen, goats, camels, pigs, cats, guanacos, lions, gnus, deer, monkeys, eagles — and 21 others) in 132 characteristic actions. The horse alone is shown in more than 40 different actions. All 3919 photographs are taken in series at speeds up to 1/6000th of a second. You will see exactly how a lion sets his foot down; how an elephant's knees are like a human's — and how they differ; the position of a kangaroo's legs in mid-leap; how an ostrich's head bobs; details of the flight of birds — and thousands of facts of motion only the fastest cameras can catch. Neither semiposed artificial shots nor distorted telephoto shots taken under adverse conditions. Artists, biologists, cartoonists, will find this book indispensable for understanding animals in motion. ''A really marvelous series of plates,'' NATURE (London). ''The dry plate's most spectacular early use was by Eadweard Muybridge,'' LIFE. 3919 photographs; 380 full pages of plates. 440pp. Printed on heavy glossy paper. Deluxe binding with headbands. 7⅞ x 10⅝. T203 Clothbound **$10.00**

THE BOOK OF SIGNS, Rudolf Koch. 493 symbols from ancient manuscripts, medieval cathedrals, coins, catacombs, pottery, etc. Crosses, monograms of Roman emperors, astrological, chemical, botanical, runes, housemarks, and 7 other categories. Invaluable for handycraft workers, illustrators, scholars, etc., this material may be reproduced without permission. 493 illustrations by Fritz Kredel. 104pp. 6⅛ x 9¼. Sewn binding.　　　　　　　　　　　　　　　　　　　　　　　　　　　T162 Paperbound **$1.00**

A HANDBOOK OF EARLY ADVERTISING ART, C. P. Hornung. The largest collection of copyright-free early advertising art ever compiled. Vol. I contains some 2,000 illustrations of agricultural devices, animals, old automobiles, birds, buildings, Christmas decorations (with 7 Santa Clauses by Nast), allegorical figures, fire engines, horses and vehicles, Indians, portraits, sailing ships, trains, sports, trade cuts — and 30 other categories! Vol. II, devoted to typography, has over 4000 speciments: 600 different Roman, Gothic, Barnum, Old English faces; 630 ornamental type faces; 1115 initials, hundreds of scrolls, flourishes, etc. This third edition is enlarged by 78 additional plates containing all new material. "A remarkable collection," PRINTERS' INK. "A rich contribution to the history of American design," GRAPHIS.
Volume 1, Pictorial Volume. Over 2000 illustrations. xlv + 242pp. 9 x 12.　　T122 Clothbound **$10.00**
Volume II, Typographical Volume. Over 4000 speciments. vii + 312pp. 9 x 12. T123 Clothbound **$10.00**
Two volume set, Clothbound, only **$18.50**

DESIGN FOR ARTISTS AND CRAFTSMEN, L. Wolchonok. The most thorough course on the creation of art motifs and designs. Create your own designs out of things around you — from geometric patterns, plants, birds, animals, humans, landscapes, and man-made objects. It leads you step by step through the creation of more than 1300 designs, ranging from near representationalism to the most advanced forms of abstraction. The material in this book is entirely new, and combines full awareness of traditional design with the work of such men as Miro, Leger, Picasso, Moore, and others. 113 detailed exercises, with instruction hints, diagrams, and details to enable you to apply Wolchonok's methods to your own work. "A great contribution to the field of design and crafts," N. Y. SOCIETY OF CRAFTSMEN. More than 1300 illustrations. xv + 207pp. 7⅞ x 10¾.　　　　　　　　　　T274 Clothbound **$4.95**

HANDBOOK OF DESIGNS AND DEVICES, C. P. Hornung. Indispensable to the designer, commercial artist, and hobbyist. It is not a text-book but a working collection of 1836 basic designs and variations, which may be used without permission. Variations of circle, line; band, triangle, square, cross, diamond, swastika, pentagon, octagon, hexagon, star, scroll, interlacement, shields, etc. Supplementary notes on the background and symbolism. "A necessity to every designer who would be original without having to labor heavily," ARTIST AND ADVERTISER. 204 plates. 240pp. 5⅜ x 8.　　T124 Clothbound **$3.95**
T125 Paperbound **$1.90**

THE UNIVERSAL PENMAN, George Bickham. This beautiful book, which first appeared in 1743 contains 212 full-page plates drawn from the work of such 18th century masters of English roundhand as Dove, Champion, and Bland. They contain 22 complete alphabets, over 2,000 flourishes, and 122 illustrations, each drawn with a stylistic grace impossible to describe. This book is invaluable to anyone interested in the beauties of calligraphy, or to any artist, hobbyist, or craftsman who wishes to use the very best ornamental handwriting and flourishes for decorative purposes. Commercial artists, advertising artists, have found it unexcelled as a source of material suggesting quality. "An essential part of any art library, and a book of permanent value," AMERICAN ARTIST. 212 plates. 224pp. 9 x 13¾.
T20 Clothbound **$10.00**

AN ATLAS OF ANATOMY FOR ARTISTS, F. Schider. A new 3rd edition of this standard text enlarged by 52 new illustrations of hands, anatomical studies by Cloquet, and expressive life studies of the body by Barcsay. 29 plates show all aspects of the skeleton, with closeups of special areas, while 54 full-page plates, mostly in two colors, give human musculature as seen from four different points of view, with cutaways for important portions of the body. 14 full-page plates provide photographs of hand forms, eyelids, female breasts, and indicate the location of muscles upon models. 59 additional plates show how great artists of the past utilized human anatomy! Michelangelo, Leonardo da Vinci, Goya, and 15 others. This is a lifetime reference work which will be one of the most important books in any artist's library. "The standard reference tool," AMERICAN LIBRARY ASSOCIATION. "Excellent," AMERICAN ARTIST. Third enlarged edition. 189 plates, 647 illustrations. xxvi + 192pp. 7⅞ x 10⅝.
T241 Clothbound **$6.00**

FOUNDATIONS OF MODERN ART, A. Ozenfant. An illuminating discussion of the interrelationship of all forms of human creativity, from painting to science, writing to religion. The creative process is explored in all facets of art, from paleolithic cave painting to modern French painting and architecture, and the great universals of art are isolated. Expressing its countless insights in aphorisms accompanied by carefully selected illustrations, this book is itself an embodiment in prose of the creative process. Enlarged by 4 new chapters. 226 illustrations. 368pp. 6⅛ x 9¼.　　　　　　T215 Paperbound **$1.95**

AN ATLAS OF ANIMAL ANATOMY FOR ARTISTS, W. Ellenberger, H. Baum, H. Dittrich. The largest, richest animal anatomy for artists available in English. 99 detailed anatomical plates of such animals as the horse, dog, cat, lion, dear, seal, kangaroo, flying squirrel, cow, bull, goat, monkey, hare, and bat. Surface features are clearly indicated, while progressive beneath-the-skin pictures show musculature, tendons, and bone structure. Detailed cross-sections are given for heads and important features. The animals chosen are representative of specific families so that a study of these anatomies will provide knowledge of hundreds of related species. "Highly recommended as one of the very few books on the subject worthy of being used as an authoritative guide," DESIGN. Second revised, enlarged edition with new plates from Cuvier, Stubbs, etc. 288 illustrations. 153pp. 11⅜ x 9.
T82 Clothbound **$6.00**

ANIMAL ANATOMY AND PSYCHOLOGY, C. R. Knight. 158 studies of the artistic aspects and individual traits which characterize a wide variety of vertebrates and invertebrates. The author, a noted animal artist, provides detailed and fascinating insights into the personality of such animals as the gorilla, mandrill, bear, bison, dromedary, camel, peccary, kangaroo, vulture, pelican, hornbill, iguana, shark, crab, and many others. Distinctive features such as eye movements, lip contour under various emotions such as fear, curiosity, or hunger, positional differences during attack and defense, horn formation, stride, and hundreds of other characteristics are clearly described and illustrated. "An excellent reference work," SAN FRANCISCO CHRONICLE. 158 illustrations. vii + 149pp. 10½ x 8¼.   T426 Paperbound **$1.75**

PRIMITIVE ART, Franz Boas. A great American anthropologist covers the entire gamut of primitive art. Pottery, leatherwork, metal work, stone work, wood, basketry, etc. Theories of primitive art, historical depth in art history, technical virtuosity, unconscious levels of patterning, symbolism, styles, literature, music, dance, etc. For laymen, the anthropologist, artist, handycrafter (hundreds of unusual motifs), and the historian. Over 900 illustrations (50 ceramic vessels, 12 totem poles, etc., etc.). 376pp. 5⅜ x 8.
T25 Paperbound **$1.95**

ON THE LAWS OF JAPANESE PAINTING, H. Bowie. Based on 9 years of profound study-experience in the late Kano art of Japan; the most authentic guide to the spirit and technique of Japanese painting. A wealth of data on control of the brush; practice exercises; manufacture of ink, brushes, colors; the use of various lines and dots to express moods. Best possible substitute for lessons from a great oriental master. 66 plates with 220 illustrations. Index. xv + 117pp. 6⅛ x 9¼.   T30 Paperbound **$1.95**

THE CRAFTSMAN'S HANDBOOK, Cennino Cennini. The finest English translation of IL LIBRO DELL' ARTE, a 15th century Florentine introduction to art technique. It is both fascinating reading and a wonderful mirror of another culture for artists, art students, historians, social scientists, or anyone interested in details of life some 500 years ago. While it is not an exact recipe book, it gives direction for such matters as tinting papers, gilding stone, preparation of various hues of black, and many other useful but nearly forgotten facets of the painter's art. 4 illustrations. xxvii + 142pp. D. V. Thompson translator. 6⅛ x 9¼.   T54 Clothbound **$3.50**

THE BROWN DECADES, Lewis Mumford. The "buried renaissance" of the post-Civil War period. He demonstrates that it contained the seeds of a new integrity and power and documents his study with detailed accounts of the founding of modern architecture in the work of Sullivan, Richardson, Root, Roebling; landscape development of Marsh, Olmsted, and Eliot; the graphic arts of Homer, Eakins, and Ryder. 2nd revised enlarged edition. Bibliography. 12 illustrations. Index. xiv + 266pp. 5⅜ x 8.
T200 Paperbound **$1.65**

STIEGEL GLASS, F. W. Hunter. Acclaimed and treasured by librarians, collectors, dealers and manufacturers, this volume is a clear and entertaining account of the life, early experiments, and final achievements in early American glassware of "Baron" Stiegel. An 18th century German adventurer and industrialist, Stiegel founded an empire and produced much of the most highly esteemed early American glassware. His career and varied glassware is set forth in great detail by Mr. Hunter and a new introduction by Helen McKearin provides details revealed by later research. "This pioneer work is reprinted in an edition even more beautiful than the original," ANTIQUES DEALER. "Well worth reading," MARYLAND HISTORICAL MAGAZINE. Introduction. 171 illustrations; 12 in full color. xxii + 338pp. 7⅞ x 10¾.
T128 Clothbound **$10.00**

THE HUMAN FIGURE, J. H. Vanderpoel. Every important artistic element of the human figure is pointed out in minutely detailed word descriptions in this classic text and illustrated as well in 430 pencil and charcoal drawings. Thus the text of this book directs your attention to all the characteristic features and subtle differences of the male and female (adults, children, and aged persons), as though a master artist were telling you what to look for at each stage. 2nd edition, carefully revised and enlarged by George Bridgman. Foreword. 430 illustrations. 143pp. 6⅛ x 9¼.   T432 Paperbound **$1.45**

PINE FURNITURE OF EARLY NEW ENGLAND, R. H. Kettell. A rich understanding of one of America's most original folk arts. 413 illustrations of more than 300 chairs, benches, racks, beds, cupboards, mirrors, shelves, tables, and other furniture show all the simple beauty and character of early New England furniture. 55 detailed drawings carefully analyze outstanding pieces. "With its rich store of illustrations, this book emphasizes the individuality and varied design of early American pine furniture. It should be welcomed," ANTIQUES. 413 illustrations and 55 working drawings. 475pp. 8 x 10¾.
T145 Clothbound **$10.00**

MASTERPIECES OF FURNITURE IN PHOTOGRAPHS AND MEASURED DRAWINGS, V. C. Salomonsky. Collectors of antiques and craftsmen know that the best possible aids to intelligent and successful furniture collecting and building are careful photographs plus detailed measured drawings. Photographs and drawings (accurate to 1/16th of an inch) of 101 exceptional pieces of furniture. Renaissance chairs and tables; Chippendale chairs, stools, etc.; Louis XV arm chairs; Queen Anne settee; Sheraton style of window seat and chairs; Hepplewhite card tables, dressing tables, sideboards; chests, secretaries, highboys, mirrors, clocks, etc., from the Jacobean to Louis XVI, Duncan Phyfe, Pembroke, and other styles. Complete information on traditions, materials, characteristics, history, etc., of each piece. "Invaluable as a reference book for students or as a guide to craftsmen," CRAFT HORIZONS. 102 photographs, over 500 drawings. Bibliography. 224pp. 7⅞ x 10¾.   T234 Clothbound **$6.00**

BASIC BOOKBINDING, A. W. Lewis. Enables the beginner and the expert to apply the latest and most simplified techniques to rebinding old favorites and binding new paperback books. Complete lists of all necessary materials and guides to the selection of proper tools, paper, glue, boards, cloth, leather, or sheepskin covering fabrics, lettering inks and pigments, etc. You are shown how to collate a book, sew it, back it, trim it, make boards and attach them in easy step-by-step stages. Author's preface. 261 illustrations with appendix. Index. xi + 144pp. 5⅜ x 8.   T169 Paperbound **$1.35**

DESIGN MOTIFS OF ANCIENT MEXICO, J. Enciso. 766 superb designs from Aztec, Olmec, Totonac, Maya, and Toltec origins. Plumed serpents, calendrical elements, wind gods, animals, flowers, demons, dancers, monsters, abstract ornament, and other designs. More than 90% of these illustrations are completely unobtainable elsewhere. Use this work to bring new barbaric beauty into your crafts or drawing. Originally $17.50. 766 illustrations, thousands of motifs. 192pp. 7⅞ x 10¾.   T84 Paperbound **$1.85**

AFRICAN SCULPTURE, Ladislas Segy. First publication of a new book by the author of critically acclaimed AFRICAN SCULPTURE SPEAKS. 163 full-page plates illustrating masks, fertility figures, ceremonial objects, etc., representing the culture of 50 tribes of West and Central Africa. Over 95% of these works of art have never been illustrated before. A 34 page introduction explains the anthropological, psychological, and artistic values of African sculpture. "Mr. Segy is one of its top authorities," NEW YORKER. 164 full-page photographic plates. Bibliography. 244pp. 6 x 9.   T396 Paperbound **$2.00**

PETS

THE CARE AND BREEDING OF GOLDFISH, Anthony Evans. Hundreds of important details about indoor and outdoor pools and aquariums; the history, physical features and varieties of goldfish; selection, care, feeding, health and breeding — with a special appendix that shows you how to build your own goldfish pond. Enlarged edition, newly revised. Bibliography. 22 full-page plates; 4 figures. 128pp. 5 x 7¼.   T920 Paperbound **75¢**

THE CARE OF CATS, K. Wilson and A. Webb. Practical advice on housebreaking, feeding, grooming, breeding, breaking cats of furniture scratching, collars, grass, many other subjects. From Abyssinians to Siamese, cats in art and folklore are discussed. 3 chapters on neutering, lice, worms, distemper, bad breath, colds, rabies, etc. Bibliography. 55 illustrations, some by famous artists. 105pp. 5 x 7¼.   T912 Paperbound **65¢**

OBEDIENCE TRAINING FOR YOUR DOG, C. Wimhurst. You can teach your dog to heel, retrieve, sit, jump, track, climb, refuse food, etc. Covers house training, developing a watchdog, obedience tests, working trials, police dogs. "Proud to recommend this book to every dog owner who is attempting to train his dog," says Blanche Saunders, noted American trainer, in her Introduction. Index. 34 photographs. 122pp. 5 x 7¼.   T938 Paperbound **75¢**

AQUARIUMS, A. Evans. Instructions on building aquariums at home: glass and cement, aerating, heating, electric wiring, etc. How to stock with waterplants; the care, breeding, diseases and difficulties of fish rearing; fish communities, and other topics. Covers tropical fish (including seahorses), goldfish, coldwater fish, and how to build, stock and maintain outdoor garden ponds. "The best small book in English on aquariums and general aquarium care," AQUARIUM JOURNAL. 115 illustrations. Bibliography. Index. 115pp. 5 x 7¼.   T900 Paperbound **65¢**